Labrador, a reader's guide

by **Robin McGrath**

Labrador, a reader's guide

by **Robin McGrath**

ISBN 978-1-7782193-1-3

Text and illustrations by Robin McGrath.
Cover by Morgen Mills and Vanessa Iddon of Perfect Day.
Design, layout, and editing by Brack and Brine.

Printed in Canada by Marquis Book Printing.
Published by Brack and Brine.

This book includes new revisions of previously published material for which Robin McGrath is the copyright holder. Brack and Brine acknowledges this publication history and the roles of other publishers and periodicals in making it possible. Detailed acknowledgements of all previous versions are documented within.

Inquiries regarding *Labrador, A Reader's Guide* may be directed to:
Brack and Brine
PO Box 1713 Stn B
Happy Valley-Goose Bay, NL
A0P 1E0 Canada

www.brackandbrine.com

Library and Archives Canada Cataloguing in Publication

Title: Labrador, a reader's guide / by Robin McGrath.
Names: McGrath, Robin, author.
Description: Includes bibliographical references and index.
Identifiers: Canadiana 20230566162 | ISBN 9781778219313
Subjects: LCGFT: Essays. | LCGFT: Reviews.
Classification: LCC PS8575.G73 L33 2023 | DDC C814/.54—dc23

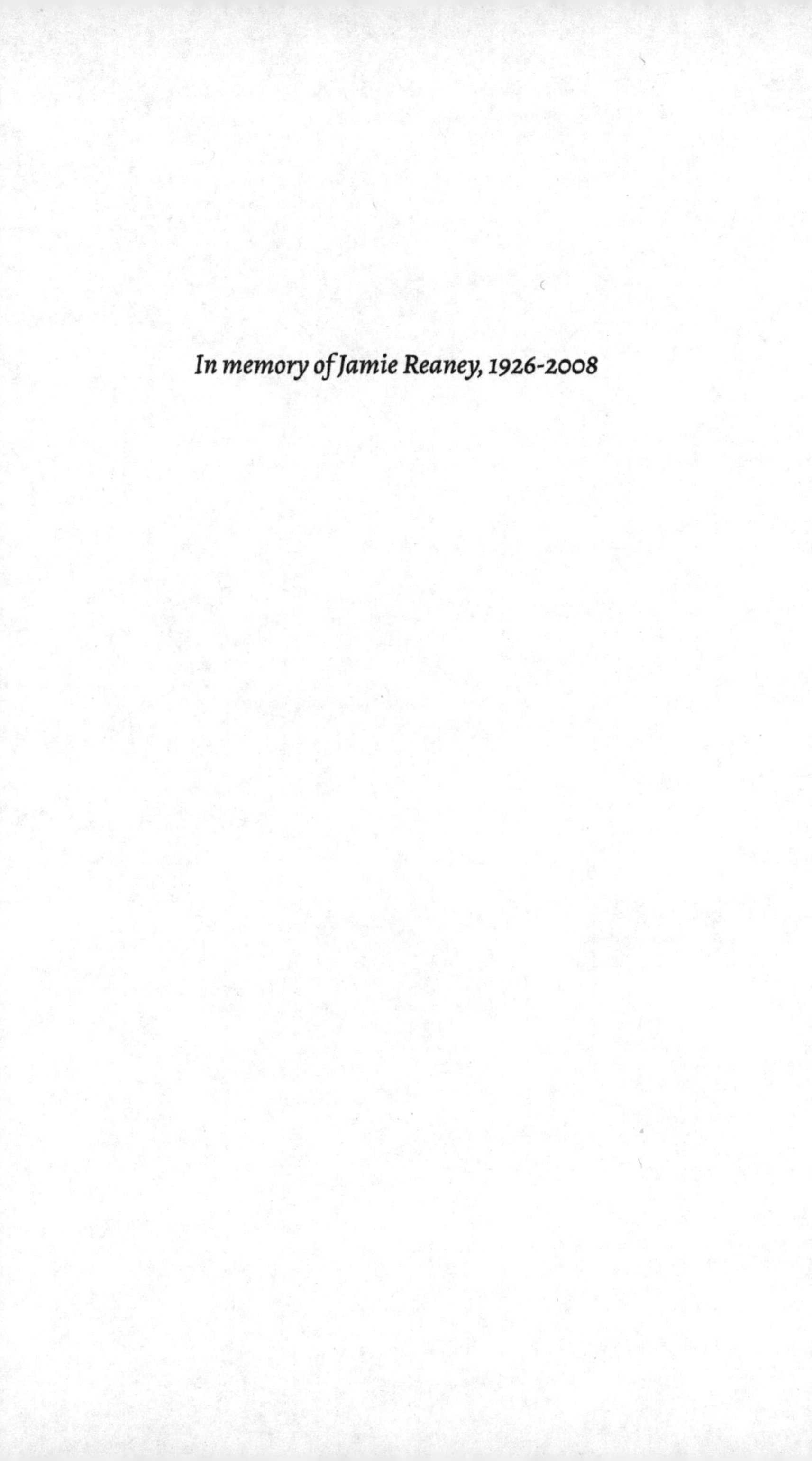

In memory of Jamie Reaney, 1926-2008

Contents

INTRODUCTION

THIS is a book about books about Labrador. I was twenty-four when I made my first trip to the Canadian Arctic in 1973, and it opened up a whole new world of reading to me. I'd been a voracious reader since childhood. Now my reading suddenly included such authors as Knud Rasmussen, Peter Freuchen, Helge Ingstad, Sheila Burnford, Jean Briggs, Vilhjalmur Stefansson, and Wilfred Grenfell.

At first, my subsequent trips into the north were working holidays. Each time, I would find some temporary job to pay my way, working at a craft store, cooking for a construction crew, or writing stories for a newspaper or magazine, but then I accidentally tripped over something that really caught my imagination.

One spring I managed to hitchhike along with a group of Inuit who were travelling by snowmobile from what is now called Taloyoak to Gjoa Haven to solidify a betrothal between two young people who had been promised in marriage at birth. The two adolescents had been born in the same camp but had not seen each other since, so this was an opportunity for the families to get together and give the young people a chance to get to know one another. The distance across the ice was about 120 kilometres, but unfortunately, the weather turned, the journey took much longer than anyone expected, we ran out of food except for an old piece of dried seal meat someone found in the bottom of a tool box, and we got very wet and cold before finally managing to locate the community.

It was probably the seal meat that did us in. Quite a few of us got very sick, and the old grandfather who was our navigator became so dehydrated he nearly died. I was fortunate enough to be taken in by the widow of one of the Porters, an Inuit family that had immigrated from Alaska in the 1930s, and though I spoke no Inuktitut and Mrs. Porter spoke little or no English, she was kind enough to search out some reading material for me as I began to recover. It mostly consisted of church magazines, old newsletters, and schoolbooks of one sort and another, but it was a welcome diversion.

Back at home, I found that despite my rather uneven transcript and my three children, my part-time studies had finally managed to earn me an honours degree in English from Western University and a scholarship to graduate school. One of my professors, James Reaney, saw me in the corridor outside the department office, stopped to congratulate me, and asked me what I was going to work on. I admitted that I hadn't much interest in the usual literary topics and probably wouldn't be taking up the opportunity to continue studying. "Well, what are you interested in?" he asked. "Inuit," I answered. Or, given the era, I probably said "Eskimos." "They have literature, too," he declared.

That simple and obvious answer poleaxed me. I thought about the hundreds of legends published in anthropology reports and collections, and of Mrs. Porter's church bulletins and newsletters with their stories, letters to the editors, and poems, and I knew right away that if I could find more of these sorts of publications, I could lay the foundation for a study of Inuit literature as it was transitioning from an oral to a written tradition. Dr. Reaney reluctantly agreed to supervise me, and a year and a bit later the Department of Indian and Northern Affairs published my master's thesis and even paid me for it. Mel Hurtig in Edmonton published my first book, a collection of Inuit Literature I titled *Paper Stays Put*, and after another four years of hard work and Arctic travel, I was able to hold in my hands a copy of my doctoral thesis, *Canadian Inuit Literature: The Development of a Tradition*, published by the Museum of Man in Ottawa. To be honest, I think I just lucked into the right topic at the right time.

Although in the course of my research I had travelled all over the Canadian Arctic and Alaska, the one place I had never been was Labrador. My father, my three brothers, and one of my seven sisters had all worked in Labrador at one time or another, and my mother had visited there, but I'd never set foot in the place. Part of the reason was that one of my brothers was by then the senior civil servant there and although we were fond of one another, we didn't agree politically. The other reason was that many of my contacts came through research and work I'd done at Indian and Northern Affairs in Ottawa, and because of Newfoundland's particular terms of Confederation, Ottawa didn't have much to do with Indigenous people in Labrador.

I did a short stint as an Associate Professor at the University of Alberta, where I taught Canadian literature and children's literature, but like many Newfoundlanders, as soon as my children were self-supporting, I bolted for home. In short order, I found myself tangled up with a man who'd been in kindergarten with me. As it happened, he travelled to Labrador for work as a lawyer, and in no time at all, he brought me to Davis Inlet and married me there. That was more than twenty-five happy years ago.

I had all this time been reading books about Labrador that came my way, starting with Elizabeth Goudie's *Woman of Labrador*, which my mother had read before it was published, sitting at Mrs. Goudie's kitchen table. I was one of the original subscribers when Doris Saunders began editing *Them Days* magazine in 1975, and I have kept up my subscription ever since. However, when my husband was appointed a Provincial Court Judge and we moved to Happy Valley-Goose Bay, I started to do serious catch-up on my Labrador reading.

Visitors, sojourners, and medical or religious missionaries wrote most of the Labrador books I read early on. During my residence in Labrador, however, the three main cultural groups, the livyers, the Inuit and the Innu, produced quite a few books also. Whenever possible, I tried to review these works to encourage the public to read them. Some books I would have liked to review, but I could not because I had already written assessments of them for various publishers.

There is also a piece on the diarist tradition in Labrador, particularly as it applies to Innu who had a very different experience of literacy. Elizabeth Penashue's book, *I Keep the Land Alive*, which was published in 2019, was finalized by Elizabeth and her editor at my dining room table over many months of consultation and work, which I observed with considerable interest.

Strictly speaking, the section on Lambert de Boilieu is not a review, but an exploration of a literary mystery, triggered by the isolation and boredom of the 2020 lockdown caused by the Covid pandemic. An exploration of the veracity of this book led to a second literary mystery about a little-known Labrador diarist.

Many of the pieces collected in this book have been previously published in newspapers and magazines such as the *Telegram* in St. John's, the *Newfoundland Quarterly*, *Labrador Life*, *Northeast Avalon Times*, *Portugal Cove-St. Philip's Times*, and *Newfound-*

land and Labrador Studies. An earlier version of "The Diarist Tradition" originally appeared in María Jesús Hernáez Lerena's *Pathways of Creativity in Contemporary Newfoundland and Labrador*. I have made some additions and changes, excised some repetitions, and grouped together books of similar kinds into sections. I would like to thank all my publishers who have encouraged and supported me in this work, and Martha MacDonald for her meticulous proofreading.

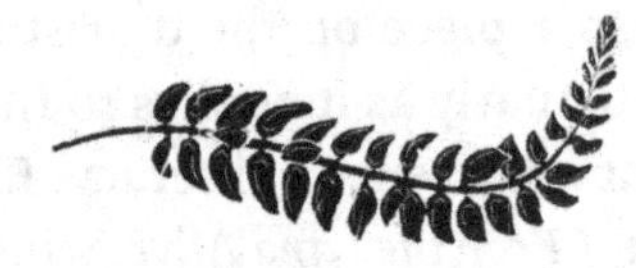

Autobiographies

Paulus Maggo; Titus Joshua and Josua Obed; Kaniuekutat and Georg Henriksen; George Rich; George Gregoire; Greta Hussey; Clarissa Smith; Josie Penny; Marilyn Churley

Fall 2000

THE appearance of Paulus Maggo's *Remembering the Years of My Life: Journeys of a Labrador Inuit Hunter* is cause for celebration. Published autobiographies by Labrador Inuit are few and far between, and this addition to a rather exclusive oeuvre is without doubt the best of its kind. Male points of view have been still more rare in the surprisingly long history of Inuit life writing in Labrador, though less so to the west. One of the first and best-known Inuit autobiographies, *I, Nuligak* by Ben Cockney, was written in the Tuktoyaktuk area in the early 1960s; *The Story of John Ayaruaq* from Rankin Inlet was published in Inuktitut in 1969; and Cape Dorset's Peter Pitseolak produced *People From Our Side* in 1975. All three books are outstanding examples of the genre, and autobiographies by Anthony Thrasher, Armand Tagoona, Levi Iqalujjuaq, Norman Eekoomiak, and others fill out the picture of life in the twentieth century for Canadian Inuit men.

Remembering the Years of My Life began its own life as a submission to the Royal Commission on Aboriginal People, whose final report was published in 1996. Paulus Maggo did fourteen tape-recorded interviews which were then transcribed, translated into English, and then translated back into the Labrador dialect of Inuktitut for his approval. The editor, Carol Brice-Bennett, readily admits that she "imposed an order on his reflections" that conveyed her own Western intellectual tradition, and she was probably right when she speculated that had Maggo written a document based on the same material, it would have been quite different. Nevertheless, she has been admirably true to his voice. Maggo shines through, not Brice-Bennett.

In all, Brice-Bennett wrote about one-third of the book, as well as assembling and editing the actual autobiography. Her contribution includes a preface outlining how the document came into being, an introduction that places Maggo's life in the context of three hundred years of Labrador history, numerous notes that clarify the central text, and an invaluable list of references. As editor, she also selected photos to complement the text. If all this seems a bit daunting, skip the preliminaries and dive straight into Maggo's world. By the time you have finished, you will be more than willing to go back and wade through a forty-page introduction for the sheer pleasure of finding out more about the man.

Maggo's voice survives transcription, translation, textual notes, and the whole complicated process of fixing words on a page. That voice is vibrant, fresh, and reasoned. Whether describing how to build a boat, regulations regarding the division of a square flipper seal, relations with Innu trappers and Newfoundland fishermen, or the decline of the Moravian church in Labrador, he is clear, confident, and compelling in his narrative. The text is similar enough to other Inuit autobiographies to be convincing, and different enough to convey a sense of his personality.

With *Remembering the Years of My Life*, Paulus Maggo has joined the ranks of contact-era Inuit who define the twentieth century in Canada's North, and Brice-Bennett joins the ranks of such collaborators as Dorothy Harley Eber and Maurice Métayer who have had the modesty and the ability to liberate Indigenous voices for future generations of all cultures. This is probably the single most important book published out of Labrador in the twentieth century: a fine way to finish off the millennium and a benchmark for the twenty-first century.

October 2014

Until recently, there weren't many early texts by Labrador Inuit storytellers available to English readers. The 18th- and 19th-century Moravian *Periodical Accounts* occasionally carried letters or stories from Hebron or Nain, and in 1894 the St. John's *Eve-*

ning Herald published extracts from the diaries of 75-year-old Lydia Campbell. Abraham Ulrikab's 1880 diary was not published until 1981.

The first regular outlets for Inuit writers were the newspaper *kinatuinamot illengajuk* and the magazine *Them Days,* both founded in the 1970s. Since then, however, Indigenous memoirs and autobiographies have proliferated, and Labrador Inuit have given us the works of Josephine Kalleo, Paulus Maggo, Dorothy Mesher, Elizabeth Goudie, and others. The scarcity of earlier Inuit memoirs made *Memories from Northern Labrador* by Titus Joshua and Josua Obed all the more welcome in 2014. Tape-recorded some time prior to Titus Joshua's death in 1972, this collection is almost all we have of the history and stories of that area from the first half of the 20th-century. It also gives us two more male voices in the predominantly female field of Labrador memoir.

Memories from Northern Labrador is a rather odd book, as it seems to transcribe raw recordings without much interference. The original Inuttitut tapes and transcriptions were lost when the Torngâsok Cultural Centre archive burned to the ground. However, an English translation was eventually found to have survived in Goose Bay. The English was retranslated into Inuttitut, and both texts have been published in a back-to-back, bilingual, hardcover edition.

Joshua and Obed were the same age and obviously got on well, but you could hardly find two more different personality types. Both had traditional upbringings, but Joshua was a rather worldly person, having spent sixteen years working at the 5 Wing Air Force Base in Goose Bay, while Obed was highly religious and very active in church affairs. In their memoirs, they both indulge in a certain amount of old-guy crankiness, complaining about how lazy young people are today, how hard they had it in their time, and how people have let their language slip away, but they are also rather hard on themselves. Joshua, in particular, declares that he's a useless old mouth who should be thrown in the dump. But he also slyly tells us that he is being paid five dollars an hour to talk into the tape recorder. For the majority of the book, it is Joshua who takes the lead, scolding the youth, talking about his life, coming up with scraps of history, and reminding us often that he can speak English and made a good wage when he wasn't hunting.

Obed encourages him and occasionally adds a few details to the stories that he obviously knows as well as Joshua does. Obed is a much more meticulous storyteller. He often tells a story in skeleton form and then tells it again, filling out the details. The first time it might be half a page long, and the second it might be four and a half pages. He knows his dates, particularly when recounting the history of the Moravian church.

While Joshua's focus tends to be family life and domestic or hunting traditions, Obed is more interested in traditional legends. Many of these stories are known in variation throughout the circumpolar world. "Lumâ," the tale of the blind boy and the loon, is probably familiar to many Canadian school children from books and films, but here the location is given as Saglek, south of Cape Mugford. Several of the stories are less familiar, but have clear echoes of pan-Arctic legends. Joshua tells of a shaman who transformed an iceberg into an island near Nain, just as Marble Island in Hudson's Bay was formed, and there are elements of the tale of the cannibal Iggimarasugjuk and the beautiful but traitorous Navarana in other stories these old men knew.

Towards the end of the book, Obed's voice begins to dominate, and it is unclear whether this was just how the recordings were arranged after the fact, or whether he was gaining confidence. Obed's tales in this part of the book are borrowed from church parables and mostly set in England or Germany. One involves the conversion of a Jew, another a prodigal son returning from army service in India. It would be interesting to compare Obed's account of the travels of Mikak to England in 1767 with some of the Moravian versions. Most surprising is Obed's account of "The Sorcerer's Apprentice," which he apparently heard from old Rev. Hettasch. I was reminded of a version of "Ulysses and the Cyclops" that I collected in the Central Arctic after a Hungarian anthropologist had been swapping stories with the local men.

The non-standard English translation isn't a problem, as it most likely echoes the English these old men did speak, but the typographical errors and occasionally confusing modifications do intrude on the enjoyment of the text. There are errors on almost every page. You get "hole" for "hold" and "year" for "yard," some words are enjambed to produce "hisgear," "theywere," and "ababy," and apostrophes are inserted into non-possessive plurals. There is a reference to Inuit making gunpowder on a hill called Ilulitsaliugvik, and the explanation is that *ilulitsaliugvik* means "ammunition." Earlier, however, we are told that this was a place where they made arrows for battles with the Innu.

Although I found it very interesting to read a raw, untouched transcript of translations from Inuttitut, the general reader might have benefitted from an introduction and annotations by someone like Carol Brice-Bennett. Failing that, the old storytellers deserve at least a decent proofreader.

Even with its flaws, this book is a small treasure, and it is a miracle that its content was saved. Since it lacks an ISBN number, it will be hard for people to find, but it's to be hoped that in the future, someone with good editorial skills will be able to mine *Memories from Northern Labrador* for some of its hidden wealth.

Fall 2009

Over the years, there have been a great many books written about the Innu of the Labrador Peninsula, but very few of them have been written from inside the culture. In recent decades, a few have reached the public: the Davis Inlet People's Inquiry's *Gathering Voices* (1995), the anthology of Innu women's writing *It's Like the Legend* (2000), and Serge Bouchard's *Caribou Hunter: A Song of a Vanished Innu Life* (2006). *I Dreamed the Animals,* Georg Henriksen's rendition of the oral autobiography of Innu Elder Kaniuekutat, who was also known by the English name John Poker, is a fine addition to that small but important genre.

Henriksen, a Norwegian anthropologist, spent two years travelling and hunting with the Mushuau Innu in the 1960s, and later returned frequently to visit them. When Henriksen was diagnosed with terminal cancer at a relatively young age, his primary goal in seeking treatment was to buy enough time to finish what he considered his most important work, *I Dreamed the Animals.* He accomplished that goal, and in 2009 his widow and daughter went to Natuashish to launch the book, where it was received with considerable joy and celebration.

I Dreamed the Animals is the product of fifty-two hours of taped Innu-aimun recordings made in 1993 with Kaniuekutat, who was then 73 years old. The result had to be translated, transcribed, organized, and edited into a coherent text. Then, by adding introductions and footnotes, Henriksen was able to draw on his own and others' knowledge to give Kaniuekutat's words a context. The result is a dense, vital and compelling book.

Kaniuekutat was a fine story-teller. Many of the

myths and legends he tells here can be found elsewhere, but only in shortened, incomplete versions. This isn't just a collection of myths, though. Kaniuekutat explains how hunters find animals through dreams and divination, the purpose and function of the sweat lodge and shaking tent ceremonies, the feasting rules for *mukushan*, and the spheres of influence of both the Innu deities and the Christian God and Devil. He also tackles the difficult question of Innu relations with *akenashau* (non-Innu) and with one another.

One of the many subjects Kaniuekutat examines is that of writing itself, which he did not entirely trust. Henriksen had encountered that attitude before among Innu, when he was hired to collect data for land claims negotiations. The chief at that time, himself illiterate, objected when Henriksen and his Innu colleague began writing down the information they received in interviews because, he said, "writing was the same as lying, and . . . was especially used by *akenashau* people to deceive the Innu."

When he was growing up, the only book Kaniuekutat was aware of was the Bible. He believed that the Bible could be used for divination, because it was the source of the Devil, just as the Innu oral tradition was a source of the trickster Kuekuatsheu. It's possible that Kaniuekutat agreed to make a book with Henriksen in order to restore a balance of power between the Innu spirits and the white man's deities, to make a book as powerful as the Bible.

Kaniuekutat had similarly ambivalent feelings

about alcohol and snowmobiles. He thought that small quantities of alcohol could be helpful in contacting the spirits, but he personally gave up using it entirely when he was in his thirties because of the negative aspects of drinking. He thought snowmobiles also contributed to a general weakening of the Innu people, but he loved to drive and was known in the community for his control of the machine.

Some of the insights to be found in *I Dreamed the Animals* may come as a surprise to readers. Anyone who has seen the Richard White collection of Innu toys at The Rooms in St. John's will recall a homemade set of checkers with a canvas playing board. Apparently, Innu played checkers with a ferocity that is more usually associated with chess, in part because checkers were used for telling the future, and you could actually kill an opponent by beating him at checkers. It was not just a game; it was a field of spiritual battle that shamans and other powerful people used to gain ascendancy in their communities.

Another of the subjects that Kaniuekutat discusses at length is the Innu attitude towards death. Innu believe that when people die, their spirits become lonely and try to bring others with them, so every death is a very dangerous time for those who loved the departed. A child, for instance, might wish his mother or another child to join him. Kaniuekutat himself once faced death and refused to die because he was concerned that he might inadvertently take his grandson Thomas with him. In many ways, death is more frightening for those who survive than for those who die.

I Dreamed the Animals is an overtly didactic book, intended to inform not just non-Innu people but also younger Innu also about a culture in transition. However, many of the lessons Kaniuekutat has to teach are not obvious. For instance, he often touches upon the subject of interdependence between husband and wife. This message is conveyed partly through the myth of Mehutshu, who turned into a star when he found himself a single parent, and partly though a description of the division of labour between men and women. Similarly, the importance of sharing food is both illustrated in the stories and overtly encouraged.

Kaniuekutat's descriptions and explanations are not always easy to understand. The words are not difficult, and the sentences make grammatical sense, but it is often necessary to puzzle out the meaning of what is being said. Henriksen's introductions and footnotes help with this, but he takes care not to intrude on Kaniuekutat's voice and offers only tentative suggestions on how the text should be read. *I Dreamed the Animals* is a little like an overheard conversation: an exchange between Henriksen and Kaniuekutat, but also sometimes addressed to Kaniuekutat's grandson Thomas. The translator, George Gregoire, occasionally offers an insight or asks a question, and George's sister Rose also sat in on some of the interviews. When you add in the explanatory footnotes of anthropologists like Peter Armitage, it really becomes a multilayered text which not only bears repeated reading, but requires it.

Fall 2017

Innu leader George Rich is known throughout Labrador as an intelligent, active, and articulate if mercurial man. If anything political is stirring in Natuashish, Rich is sure to be on the scene. As a boy, he experienced the stressful shift to permanent housing with his formerly nomadic family, and by the time he was a teenager, life at Davis Inlet had begun to settle into a pattern of deterioration. By the time he was an adult, things were spinning out of control.

Rich's adult life was a roller-coaster ride of work, travel, and alcohol, but by 1995, he had sobered up and stabilized. It was then he decided to finish the education he had abandoned in Grade 8. He moved with his family to Happy Valley-Goose Bay and enrolled in a course of Adult Basic Education. One of the programs he participated in was called "Exploring Memory, Finding Meaning," a writing course sponsored by the National Literacy Secretariat. The student writers used photographs of people and places from their past as a way to access memories that were important to them.

With the help of photos of his community and his

family, most of which were taken by anthropologists and missionaries, Rich was able to reconstruct both good and bad experiences from his childhood and to explore how these experiences affected his later roles as a husband, father, and community leader. The manuscript, which he titled *Struggling with My Soul*, was made available in 2000 as an online autobiography, and was later published in a new print edition, updated to cover the community's resettlement from Davis Inlet to Natuashish, and with a complete revamp of the photos and design.

Struggling with My Soul is not the first Labrador Innu life story to make it into print, but it is the first of any length that has not been filtered through the mind or tape recorder of a non-Innu collaborator. Camille Fouillard's editorial hand is expert and invisible.

Newfoundland and Labrador has no literary award for book design, but if it did, *Struggling with My Soul* would surely win it, because the book is a delight to look at, to hold, and to read. Oral storytellers are often ill-served by print—the ink bleeds the life out of the author's voice. In this case, however, the photographs have been handled adeptly to convey the author's vibrancy and personality.

Bulgarian artist Vessela Brakalova took traditional Innu designs, starting with a famous ceremonial caribou robe painted by Rich's grandmother, and adapted the red, blue and yellow images to decorate and highlight certain parts of the text. Coloured finials, like decorative cast-cuts, are scattered throughout the book, and all the photographs are clearly identified. The overall effect of the design is warm and personal, closing the gap between the writer and the reader, so that Rich's stories ring with emotions of both joy and grief.

Struggling with My Soul is not a large book, running to just 90 pages, but it is an important one, giving all readers, whether young or old, Innu or not, insight into a little-known and less-understood group of Labradorians.

February 2013

George Gregoire is not well known outside Labrador, but within his own Northern community, he has had a considerable profile. He has been a band councilor in Natuashish, an interpreter for the courts, a land claims negotiator, and although never in the spotlight as his sister Elizabeth Penashue often is, he has been on the sidelines of every major political event involving the Innu over the last three decades.

Gregoire began writing *Walk with My Shadow* in 1995 with the help of a Canada Council Explorations grant. Like many novice writers, he found the task more difficult than he had expected, but he stuck with it. It probably helped that he had the support and assistance of Camille Fouillard, with whom he worked on *Gathering Voices*, the people's inquiry into the deaths of six children in a house fire in Davis Inlet in 1992.

Although *Walk with My Shadow* is subtitled "The Life of an Innu Man," it is not exactly a conventional cradle-to-grave autobiographical account. The first seventy pages or so detail Gregoire's years growing up in the bush and in the community of Sheshatshiu. The youngest in the family, he played with his sister Elizabeth, learned to hunt from his father, and occasionally attended school in Sheshatshiu, which he did not enjoy. Like most Innu children, he was forced to attend church frequently, and like most Innu adults he has not rejected all the tenets of Roman Catholicism but regrets the imposed abandonment of traditional Innu spirituality.

Gregoire has periodically struggled with alcohol abuse. Sober for long stretches—years at a time—he is well aware of his own frailty and susceptibility, and he has put that self-knowledge to use by counselling others who are trying to get and stay sober. In the book, he confesses to a number of binges since first sobering up, and admits with regret that during his drinking days he was unfaithful to his wife, but he also describes the efforts he made to straighten out and be a good parent and spouse. Such honesty is admired among the Innu and could be emulated by others in our society.

When Gregoire gets into the political life of the community, things become a little less transparent. I read this book alongside a recent work by Cyril Goodyear, and I noticed that they both adopt the same tactic of discussing civil servants and politicians by name until they come to criticize them, when they both switch into identifying them by title, such as "Former Chief of the Innu Nation" or "Deputy Minister of Northern Affairs." I had initially thought this might be an Innu convention, but maybe it's just an avoidance technique adopted by people who depend on government officials and voters for their livelihoods.

Gregoire has very decided opinions on everything, from relocation to addictions treatment to gun laws. He is quite aware that the relocation of Davis Inlet was very lucrative for southern businesspeople and that a good many consultants and contractors did very well out of it. Southern consultants, lawyers, and addictions counsellors may have good intentions, but they do make their livings off Innu grief and pain, and inevitably they have their own agendas. Sometimes they forget that they are hired to do what the Innu want, not what they think the Innu need. Gregoire is there to remind them of their priorities.

Some things in this book that Innu take for granted will come as a surprise to non-Innu readers. Band councils, for example, are expected to pay for charter flights for Innu families to go to St. John's whenever a relative is dying there. Most Innu do not pay rent for their houses. When Gregoire's truck breaks down on a trip to Labrador City, the first thing he does is call the Band Council to see if he can get them to pay half the tow. Funerals and the transportation of bodies are seen as community responsibilities, not family ones. The lives of Innu are much more communal than those of their *akenashau*, or non-Innu, neighbours.

You can learn a lot about the Innu from this book. Their spiritual bond with the land, their respect for Elders, their reliance on dreams for guidance, their attitudes towards conflicts of interest, their ability to accept contradictory religious beliefs, and their sense of obligation to share food and equipment, are all complex ideas that are unfamiliar to most non-Innu.

You can also learn a little Innu-aimun, since Gregoire uses the Innu words for some common concepts that are more subtle than their English counterparts, including Nitassinan for the Innu homeland, *utshimau* for boss or leader, and *nutshimit* for the bush or country. Hang around with the Innu long enough, and you begin to realize that these are highly charged and subtle words that evoke different emotions in Innu-aimun than they do in English.

I don't agree with everything George Gregoire writes in this book. For example, he says that Davis Inlet "was a beautiful place to live." Maybe fifty years ago it was, but even twenty-five years ago it wasn't. Half the trees on the island had been burned down, the landscape was littered with Styrofoam and disposable diapers, the ground was denuded of grass so any movement kicked up clouds of dust, and there was raw sewage everywhere. Maybe he meant that the island could have been beautiful if it hadn't been overpopulated and overused.

More puzzling to me is his assertion that Innu parents are not able to control their children, because "we just couldn't punish them anymore because if we did, we'd end up in jail . . . We couldn't touch our children because of government laws." In over forty years of working with and living with Indigenous people, I never once saw a First Nations or Inuk parent physically discipline a child. I never saw them revoke privileges, berate, or in any other way enforce discipline on a child except perhaps by teasing or, at worst, withdrawing attention and approval.

On the whole, though, almost all of what Gregoire says about white betrayal, racism, and dishonesty towards the Innu is true. At best, *akenashau* ignored the Innu and their rights; at worst, they negotiated in bad faith. This comes through in one anecdote in which Gregoire describes how an Elder, appointed to negotiate land rights, realized that he wasn't there to negotiate how much land the Innu were going to give the *akenashau*, but how much they were going to be allowed to keep.

Gregoire's book is a breath of fresh air, a rare window into the lives of people alongside whom the majority of Newfoundlanders and Labradorians have lived for hundreds of years, but about whom they still know very little.

*

August 2011

Greta Hussey's *Our Life on Lear's Room, Labrador* first came out in 1981. I encountered it initially in reprint some years ago and was charmed by the work. It is a short book and a fast read, but the content is not thin. In fact, it's stuffed so full of detail that it's hard to believe it came straight from the author's memory.

Each summer for sixteen years, young Greta Lear sailed to the Labrador from Port de Grave, first as a small child accompanying her parents and later as a cook for a fishing crew. The Lears worked hard and did without a great deal all through the Great Depression, but they didn't go hungry. Family affection, curiosity, an adventurous nature, and access to books made up for any deficiencies in Greta's diet and clothing.

Although Hussey makes it clear that the Lears' experiences weren't necessarily typical for coastal settler and Newfoundland families, she herself seemed to have led a charmed childhood and youth that left her with wonderful memories of neighbours, the landscape, and the practices of everyday life.

Whether recounting the various games she played as a child, describing how to "make do" by reversing sleeves in a sweater or mending a pot with an old rag, recalling the births and deaths in the community, or describing the duties of the crew cooks, she brings insight, energy, and affection into all she writes. She can number and describe the windows in their house, the panes of glass in the windows, the operation of each latch on each door, the lamps, mats and beds, and how they were constructed, cleaned, mended, used. And her account is never boring, only full of fascinating detail.

If you haven't come across this lovely little memoir, or even if you have, it is well worth the price. It is uplifting without being saccharine or sentimental.

April 2010

Broken Wings tells the story of Clarissa Smith, who grew up on the Quebec-Labrador border in the 1950s. The oldest girl in a large family, with a feckless father and a dissolute mother, Smith was pressed into servitude early in life. When her mother developed cancer, she was burdened with the task of caring for five younger siblings. Smith was thirteen when her mother died, and for two years she was almost solely responsible for the care and maintenance of these children.

By 1963, ground down by poverty, ignorance, and work, Smith came unstuck, and social services finally stepped in. The younger children were placed in foster homes, and Smith spent some time in hospital recovering from the emotional and physical neglect and abuse she had suffered. She was later sent to a boarding school in Coaticook, Quebec, which turned her life around.

The style of *Broken Wings* is somewhat extreme and riddled with clichés ("My marriage had dissipated like footprints in the sand when the tide rolls on shore"), and the prose isn't helped by the extensive use of spelled pronunciation ("We're aw gonna starbe t'deat, jest like Mum sed") or by the numerous grammatical and typographical errors. However, there is such energy and passion in the telling of the story that it's hard not to be caught up in it.

Smith could have benefitted from a good editor, and even a good proofreader would have helped. Fans of Shirley Murphy's *Allan Square* will probably like *Broken Wings*, as it has many of the same qualities, both good and bad. If this work were re-edited, it could be a fine, powerful book.

December 2010

So Few on Earth: A Labrador Métis Woman Remembers is a book that is difficult to like yet impossible not to admire. Josie Curl Penny grew up at Spotted Island and Cartwright in the 1940s and 50s, and describes her poverty-stricken early childhood in a large family in near-idyllic terms, placing them in stark contrast to her two years at Lockwood School run by the International Grenfell Association. When her family moved to Cartwright, Penny changed schools and lived at home, but by then her bond with her parents had been damaged beyond repair, and she became a rebellious and promiscuous teenager.

Penny's parents had both Inuit and white heritage. The term Métis, which generally refers to a specific Indigenous people with historical homelands in Western Canada, was used for a time in Labrador (with and without the accent) to refer to people of mixed Inuit-European heritage, though the Labrador Metis Nation has since been re-formed as the NunatuKavut Community Council, on a different cultural basis. Despite the presence of "Métis" in the subtitle, there is no discussion in this book of the social or political implications of being a mixed-race Labradorian. In fact, Penny makes only one or two passing references to her heritage, so anyone looking to this memoir for information or insight into NunatuKavut culture will have to dig deep to find it.

That isn't to say that the memoir isn't an important record of the NunatuKavummiut experience, just that the discussion is not overt. The impact of residential schools on Indigenous people in Canada has been huge, and much of this book's content reflects stories I have heard from across the Arctic and southern Canada: mindless regimentation, insensitive treatment, humiliating tactics, thoughtless manipulation, and sexual abuse.

Though sexual abuse is what most people (and law courts) focus on, this book makes it clear that many crimes other than rape were also perpetrated against Indigenous children, including starving them of affection and approval and alienating them from their families.

Penny was gang-raped twice by boys at Lockwood when she was nine years old. I know a woman of similar heritage who says the same happened to her at a residential school in Aklavik when she was a mere six years of age. She spent a week in the infirmary, where nobody ever spoke to her about what had happened, and then was returned to the dormitory and classes without any further mention of the incident. These terrible things happened, and the sexual abuse of children by fellow students is still a taboo subject in the Indigenous world, so it was certainly brave of Penny to write about it.

Much of the book is simply a description of daily life on the Labrador coast: the work, the food, the accidents and illnesses, the seasonal move to winter houses. Small children die, more children are born, a brother drowns, and the Americans turn up to seduce the locals, literally and figuratively. There isn't exactly a lot of plot development in this book, but enough happens to keep a reader turning the pages.

There are quite a number of factual errors, such as confusing the BCG inoculation for tuberculosis with a scratch test, and the sections on Grenfell, the *Kyle*, and Lockwood School itself read like they've been lifted from an encyclopedia rather than from her memory. But these are minor problems.

The real fly in the ointment is the dialogue and the way it undermines a reader's faith in the author. It's bad enough that Penny recreates long passages of dialogue that she could not possibly have remembered, but she also does it in the most demeaning manner. "I'm goin hunting tomarra marnin," says her father. "Weers ya goin?" replies her mother. "Bawling" is rendered as "ballin," "month" is "mont," and words like "these" and "those" are rendered as "deze" and "doze."

Penny quotes in its entirety a letter her mother wrote to the house mother at Lockwood School, which includes such lines as "Josie wants de go de school terrible bad, and she pees in her overalls when she got a peer on . . ." It's unlikely the author would have had the letter, and even less likely that her mother, who had a grade three education, would have been able to spell "overalls" and "terrible" but could not manage the word "to."

I am not referring to the use of dialect, I am concerned about spelled pronunciation. When Penny quotes American servicemen or British teachers, she does not try to spell their accents, but when quoting the supposedly quaint, uneducated Labradorians, she does, making them sound ignorant, inarticulate and backward. In case anyone reading this thinks I'm being unfair to an otherwise brave and articulate writer, I should point out that Penny changed perfectly good published material to conform to her own bizarre notions of what Labradorians should sound like on paper. At one point she quotes from Stewart Holwell, who was interviewed by *Them Days* magazine.

According to Penny, Stewart said, "I used ta carry de mail from Buckle's Point ta Battle Harbour for

$200 a winter . . . Now, de people along de coast were good ta us and dey took turns feedin us." I looked up the interview, and it actually read, "I used to carry the mail from Buckle's Point to Battle Harbour for two hundred dollars a winter . . . Now, the people along the coast were good, we paid nothing for our meals or board or even meal for our dogs, people took turns feeding us." Reads differently, doesn't it?

As a Labradorian herself, who took her grade seven education to McMaster University, Penny probably did not mean to demean Labradorians, and I can only think that someone at the McMaster Creative Writing Course she took gave her some very bad advice. That's unfortunate, because this is a book that deserves attention.

April 2014

On the Goose, Josie Penny's second volume of memoirs, published two years later, indicates that she and her publishers learned very little from the publication of her first book. *On the Goose* contains just as many typos and grammatical errors, but is far less compelling than her first volume. Published by Dundurn Press, *On the Goose* is the story of Penny's life in Goose Bay as a young married woman with four small children, a series of demanding jobs, and an abusive, alcoholic husband. The raw material is inherently interesting, but the really good bits are buried under a mountain of bland, pointless detail. There's a whole chapter on family pets and another on a camping trip she took with her family, compete with menus. There are also chunks of historical background that, again, sound like they were lifted from an encyclopedia.

One of the more irritating techniques Penny uses to move things along involves literally hundreds of rhetorical questions clustered throughout the text. "Where was I going? What was I doing here? What was happening to me?" or "What was life all about? How did I end up in an abusive marriage? Was I not smart enough to see what was coming?" My rhetorical question for the author is "Why are you asking me?" These are questions a book is supposed to answer.

Whenever she runs out of something to say and needs to clew up a chapter, Penny resorts to tears, idle tears. She tells us that she "murmured through my tears" and wept "tears of joy," that some "tears trickled down his cheeks" while others were "cried silently into my pillow," and so on. There are enough tears here to refloat the old *Kyle*, so many that their effect totally dissipates.

Penny is trying to tell the story of an insecure but plucky little girl making good in life through hard work and determination, as well as the story of a boom town that grew up in the wilderness. Sometimes her assumed naïveté is a bit hard to swallow, especially when it is written in spelled-pronunciation. "Wass dat black stuff on de road?" she asks when she sees pavement for the first time. "Wass it dere for?" This is coming from a seventeen-year-old who claims to have been a voracious reader of books and movie magazines.

On the Goose shares the "A Labrador Métis Woman Remembers" subtitle with Penny's earlier memoir, so you would expect it to contain some reference to her Indigenous heritage. There is none, nor is there any discussion of racism—and you can't tell me there wasn't racism in Goose Bay in the 1960s. There is no discussion at all of Penny's Inuit heritage. In fact, I don't think there's even a mention of race or Inuit in the entire book, except for the subtitle.

The manuscript was edited by Penny's daughter, who we are told had just finished a four-year degree at McMaster. McMaster is a good university, but a university degree does not make you into an editor. There are dozens of ill-chosen or incorrect words to stumble over, beginning early on where Penny writes "Cartwright" when she means "Goose Bay" and "Natuashish" when she means "Sheshatshiu." She misspells names such as Warr, Rompkey, and Finta, and Nurse Susan was British, not German.

On the Goose makes a great argument for the use of professional editors. A proper editor would have cut this book down by a third, checked names, corrected grammar, removed repetitions, and probably spotted most of the typos. A real editor wouldn't have turned this into a great book, but certainly would have turned it into a better one.

As Penny says in the front of the book, this is her

story as she saw and remembered it. However, that's no excuse for not checking facts that are easily established. Hamilton River Road does not go east towards DOT Hill and the docks, it goes west. Warr's Pharmacy opened in 1964, not 1961. The docks were a civilian operation, not a military one. The list of errors is long and the errors themselves are unnecessary.

Even a bad book takes a lot of time and effort to write. I don't blame the author for the poor production. I blame the publishers, who have a responsibility to protect their writers from criticism such as this. As a reader or as a writer, you have a right to a properly edited book with few typographical errors, no unnecessary repetitions, and a minimum of purple prose and clichés.

Every few weeks I get a phone call or an email from some hopeful author, asking about publishers. Usually they have been lured by some online scam-artist who promises they will edit, print, market, and promote their book. Buyer beware. *On the Goose* goes to show that even legitimate publishers, like plumbers, do not always do good work.

May 2015

According to former Ontario cabinet minister Marilyn Churley, the author of *Shameless*, a million women in Canada have "lost their children to adoption." Accounting for birth parents and adoptive parents, that suggests that around five million parents and children are directly impacted by legislation related to adoption disclosure in this country. Churley, who grew up in Goose Bay, was an unmarried teenager when she found herself pregnant and alone in 1968, essentially forced to give up her child. The social welfare system wouldn't assist her unless she disclosed her situation to her parents back home, and because she knew her conservative father would be enraged and wounded, she chose to go it alone.

Fast forward a couple of decades or so, and Churley found herself the Registrar General of Ontario, the province in which she had given up her child. The frustration she felt when her duties included cutting the ribbon on a new Government Services births and deaths records office reminded me of the crowd that gathered after the building containing the births and deaths records storage vault on Harvey Road in St. John's burned to the ground. The tension was palpable as bystanders waited to see if the records had survived the inferno.

Shameless is Churley's account of the loss and recovery of her son, and of the reform of adoption disclosure legislation in Ontario and Canada. Although birth mothers' rights were the most frequently-cited reason not to release information, it is fairly clear the birth mothers suffered more from this than anyone. In Churley's words, it was "a callous and indifferent society that had shunned and shamed them," and the same society was not protecting their identities, but rather making confidentiality "a condition for surrender, not a promise."

According to Churley, it was most often middle-class, male politicians of a certain age who vociferously opposed adoption disclosure legislation, afraid perhaps that their own youthful indiscretions might come home to roost. One politician even opposed disclosure because when birth mothers were asked for the name of the birth father, "any name they gave was registered . . . There was never any check done."

A portion of *Shameless* is devoted to Churley's own life—her childhood in Labrador, her hippie years backpacking around Europe, the crash pads and squats she lived in, and the excitement of her own political awakening to social and environmental concerns. Slowly she gravitated back towards her somewhat conservative Moravian Christian family, and she morphed into a left-leaning but respectable activist and elected politician and provincial cabinet minister.

Most of the book, however, relates to adoption disclosure legislation, Churley's numerous failed attempts to get a private member's bill through the house, the various lobby groups that formed either to assist or to halt progress, and the politicians who helped or hindered along the way. Today, when out-of-wedlock pregnancies are common and open adoptions the norm, it is hard to understand the fury that surrounded these issues, but the slowness of legislative reform in general has not changed.

As an adoptive mother, I was not particularly affected by disclosure legislation, because my daughter, who was seven when I got her, was Indigenous, and Indigenous status is the one thing that supposedly isn't affected by adoption. Fortunately, I knew enough about the law to request disclosure of her original birth name (it had been changed several times), ascertain whether she was registered with her band under her new name as required by law (she wasn't), and then request and record her band number. She and I both knew that eventually she could find her birth family, which she did.

The same was not the case for the nine other adoptees in my family. Two were adopted as step-children, so presumably they could find their other birth parent if they really wanted to, and two were open adoptions, but the other five grew up not knowing their original names, whether they had other siblings, or except for what was written on their skins, their ethnic origins. I believe they all found their mothers eventually, and to the best of my knowledge, only one birth mother refused contact.

In presenting the arguments and histories of other birth mothers and adoptees, Churley's book is a good primer for potential mother-child reunions. We hear about a woman whose birth was the result of a sexual assault, another who was falsely promised she would be told where her child was when he turned 18, and a man who had two adopted sisters whom he feared to lose. Confidentiality was a central issue in many of the stories. Opponents of disclosure claimed that birth mothers had received commitments in writing from Ontario Children's Aid that their names would never be released, but Churley claims that this was a myth. "No doubt some women were given verbal assurances . . . but no such commitments were ever made in writing." In fact, mother's names were included on adoption orders up until 1969.

Churley's final chapter looks to the future and speculates about how adoption disclosure legislation might be extended to include foreign adoptions as well as sperm, egg, and embryo donors and their biological offspring. She ends with a list of resources for locating adoption information in Ontario as well as in the rest of Canada and the United States. There are at least five million people out there who might find this book a valuable resource, for thought if not for research.

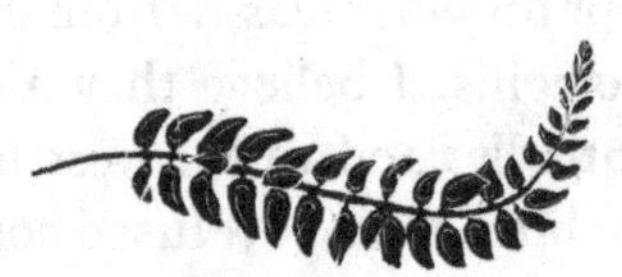

Novels

Norman Duncan; Mary Bourchier Sanford; Dillon Wallace; Nina Hepburn Dinwoodie; Julius Lips; Hammond Innes; Nevil Shute; John Wyndham; Harold Horwood; Phyllis S. Moore; John Steffler; Katherine Govier; Kathleen Winter

FOR over a century, from the mid-1800s to the mid-1900s, many different publications entitled *Boy's Own* were popular in Britain, the United States, and Canada. These books, magazines, story papers, and newsletters were aimed at preteen and teenaged boys and featured adventure tales that encouraged moral piety, physical strength, and intellectual curiosity. Because of their popularity, the phrase "Boy's Own" came to be used to describe accounts of men doing brave and exciting things.

Fiction writers began to emulate these publications' content and style to appeal to the same readership, often setting their stories in remote and exotic regions. Labrador came in for its share of the Boy's Own treatment, and it became the setting for a number of fairly successful "YA" or young adult novels, particularly after 1892 when Wilfred Grenfell began to make Labrador the focus of his attentions. In fact, Grenfell himself wrote in the Boy's Own style, and the protagonists of several of the most popular of these books were modelled after him.

Norman Duncan, a Canadian writer who worked mainly for American publications and universities, spent a summer travelling with Dr. Grenfell along the Labrador Coast. Duncan set most of his novels in Newfoundland, but *Dr. Luke of the Labrador*, which appeared in 1904, drew on his experiences from that time. Duncan denied that he based his portrait of Dr. Luke on Grenfell, but it's obvious that's exactly what he did.

The protagonist of Dr. Luke is a young medical man who wanders into Labrador as a ship's physician and is called to the deathbed of a woman who could have easily been saved had she been attended by someone with basic medical knowledge. The woman dies, and her husband, devastated by his loss, soon follows, leaving two orphaned children and a small fish-merchant business. The doctor steps in, becomes a surrogate father to the boy, and eventually falls in love with the older sister.

Dr. Luke rediscovers his Christian values through hard work, service to the community, and adventure in the open air. The story incorporates the Muscular Christianity that can also be found in Grenfell's own books, and as Patrick O'Flaherty has noted, "Grenfell's medical and missionary heroics came to embody for many writers the glamour of Labrador."

*

In the same year that *Dr. Luke* was published, another Canadian writer working in America, Mary Bourchier Sanford, produced *The Wandering Twins: A Story of Labrador*. In this tale, sixteen-year-old twins Ulrica and Ivan Steward travel from England to Wabastan, Labrador, to find their father after their guardian aunt dies. The aunt has been cheated of all her money and the twins have only enough cash to pay their way to the last place from which their father wrote them. Once there, the formerly privileged twins must rely on kindly Labradorians to help them out and teach them to work and live without servants.

Like most Boy's Own books, *The Wandering Twins* consists of a series of adventures, which includes a fall down a cliff face, being lost in a storm, an unlikely encounter with two bears, and an even unlikelier pursuit by a vicious wolf. There is the usual obligatory romantic subplot—tastefully innocent, of course—a clearly expressed disapproval of drinking and gambling, and a happy ending. Dr. Grenfell makes his guest appearance as Dr. Greville.

One unusual element in the novel is a conflict over class. Ulrica expresses affection for a young man who works as a fisherman, to which her brother objects. In keeping with the general rules of Boy's Own books, Ulrica may have a slightly more enlightened attitude to class structures, but she is also frail, timid, and generally much more fearful than her manly young twin. It's his job to look out for her physically, while it's hers to keep house for him and set his moral compass.

There are some factual errors in *The Wandering Twins* that would go unnoticed by readers unfamiliar with Labrador: a sled that is clearly a toboggan is called a komatik, cranberries take the place of redberries, and there is an Innu raid on the winterhouses in which all the Livyers' supplies are stolen. This last is an event clearly at odds with historic accounts from trappers and others, who reported that starving Innu might occasionally help themselves to food from empty cabins, but they always left some for the owners. However, Sanford must have done her homework before writing the book, as it contains fewer egregious errors than most books of its kind.

Throughout the novel, Sanford manages to short-cut familiarity with her characters by giving them a variety of different speech patterns, so the upper-class twins find everything "jolly," and a French-Canadian fisherman explains that Labradorians are self-reliant because "No shop is here, no place of some kind whatever who one the goods may buy." A kindly Irish woman observes that Ulrica is "so wor-rn out ye can hardly hould yer head up," and when a Newfoundlander urges Ulrica to jump over a large gap in a wharf, he assures her "ye'll come floatin' over on the wings o' the wind as if 't wuz yer terry firmer." These speech patterns reinforce the cultural diversity that existed in Labrador then and now.

Sanford, who had alienated some Roman Catholics with her first novel, *The Romance of a Jesuit Mission,* did somewhat better with *The Wandering Twins.*

The novel was adopted as a reader in the Kansas school system and was also approved of by Sunday schools throughout the US.

Dillon Wallace, whose life embodied the ethos of Boy's Own adventuring, wrote about a dozen books about Labrador, and although some were memoirs such as *The Lure of the Labrador Wild,* in which he described his calamitous first trip with Leonidas Hubbard, a number of the others were novels aimed at young male readers.

One of the most popular, *Bobby of the Labrador,* came out in 1916. It is like Duncan's *Dr. Luke of the Labrador* not only in title, but in the shared theme that hard work and adventure lead to a healthy mind in a healthy body. The plot is not unlike Rudyard Kipling's 1897 best-seller *Captains Courageous,* about the Grand Banks fishery. In *Bobby,* an Inuk fisherman named Abel finds a boat adrift, and upon salvaging it, he discovers a dead man and a small frightened boy on board. The child is just old enough to know his first name and little else. Abel and his wife have no children, and they decide that Bobby has been sent to them by God. They bury the dead man, tuck his papers away where they are essentially forgotten, and raise the child as their own.

The childhood of the impulsive but brave Bobby involves one close call after another, including being swept out to sea on an ice pan like Dr. Grenfell. Eventually, everything is resolved in an unlikely but happy coincidence that reunites Bobby with his birth family.

There are some anomalies present in *Bobby of the Labrador* that might not pass muster with most Labrador readers. For instance, three of the characters are attacked by a pack of wolves, and although the author cites Labradorian Job Edmunds as his source, such an event is unlikely and unprecedented. Conversely, when Bobby encounters and kills a polar bear, the reader is incorrectly assured that polar bears, "unless placed in a position where they must defend themselves, will rarely attack man." Moreover, the hunters feed the polar bear's liver to the dogs, which apparently are immune to the toxic and deadly effect it normally has upon any mammal that eats it.

Other elements of the book are not impossible, but are highly unlikely: when Bobby is swept out to sea and picked up by a sealing vessel on its way to the Front, he's able to get a bath on board the vessel, an idea most swilers would find hilarious. Additionally, Labrador Inuit of the time were much more literate than their settler neighbours, so it's unlikely that Abel would be not only unable to read, but also unaware that documents found on the body of the man in the boat might help to identify Bobby.

The racist notion that Bobby has all the intelligence and bravado of a white person and all the generosity and honesty of an Inuk really boils down to him being a better Inuk than a real Inuk or a mixed blood boy could ever be. This ethnocentric cliché can be found in a number of other novels about Labrador, such as Harold Horwood's *White Eskimo*.

Tents in the Wilderness: The Story of a Labrador Indian Boyhood, was Julius Lips's only young adult novel, his other works all being non-fiction for adults. Like many of those who wrote about Labrador, Lips and his wife spent time on the Ungava peninsula beginning in 1935, while he did ethnographic field research for his study of Innu, whom he knew as Montagnais-Naskapi Indians. Although Lips was German by birth, the Nazi program of censorship meant that Lips, a Jew, was banned from publication in his own country at that time. *Tents in the Wilderness* was first published in the United States in English in 1942. The work was not available in Germany until after the war, but it is now highly regarded there.

Like many of Dillon Wallace's Labrador books, *Tents in the Wilderness* contains only a whisper of a plot but is stuffed to the gills with "how to" information, such as how to make snowshoes and how to track animals. Young Innu boy Pirre learns various skills from his father, and the author conveys much of this information to his youthful readers. Although *Tents* is not as well-known as Lips's anthropological works for adults, it is interesting to note that Mamu

Tshishkutamashutau Innu Education lists *Tents in the Wilderness* as one of twelve books about the Innu that they recommend. In fact, they were so impressed with it that in 2015, when the work was out of copyright, they produced a second edition with glossary, corrections, and a map.

Nina Hepburn Dinwoodie's tale of a boy and his dog, *Storms on the Labrador,* came out in 1938, the same year that the first "Lassie Come Home" story appeared in the *Saturday Evening Post.* Like *Dr. Luke, Storms on the Labrador* incorporates a very modest and idealized love match for older readers, which is similarly driven by sentiment rather than sex. Here the boy protagonist has lost his father, and his widowed mother is being courted by Steve, a hard-working logging boss who is physically powerful, but who also has a fierce and uncontrollable temper. Steve gives young Finley an "Indian dog" he calls Cracky, who embodies all the faithful courage and patience that Steve lacks, and boy and dog survive a series of outdoor adventures until all comes right in the end.

An element of Dinwoodie's work that rings true when the adventures themselves stretch credibility are the illustrations, from the author's own block prints. She clearly and realistically depicts not just the landscape, but also daily activities on the coast with men straining at the oars of a dory, cleaning their catch, mending nets, dancing, and hunting on snowshoes.

Hammond Innes's 1958 best-seller, *The Land God Gave to Cain,* is not strictly speaking a boy's adventure story, but it adheres so closely to the model and contains so little that one could consider adult, that it probably only avoids the young adult classification by a hair's breadth. In this case, the boy is in his twenties, and the events of the plot are triggered by an airplane crash in the bush.

A radio distress signal is picked up by a paralyzed English war vet who dies when he attempts to respond, and his son goes to Canada to try to find the crash site and possibly rescue the survivors. Much emphasis is given to the "grimness and the lostness and the emptiness" of the land, but Innes stretches credulity when he has his young Englishman, who has never spent a night under canvas, journey alone 400 miles into the interior of the Labrador Peninsula in November without so much as a sleeping bag. There is also the obligatory love story which, as a *Kirkus* review put it, "adds only a minimal amount of anti-freeze" to the novel.

Refreshingly, however, the book takes its background from the building of the Quebec North Shore and Labrador Railway, with vivid descriptions of the work camps, the cookshacks, and the men who built the railroad under miserable conditions. Innes almost certainly visited Sept-Îles to get background for the book, but as the only trees he mentions are jack pines, he probably didn't travel up the line through Labrador, where jack pines are far from prolific. Later in life, Innes became a devoted tree planter, so he certainly would have noticed other kinds of trees if he'd seen them. The most memorable thing about *The Land God Gave to Cain* is its title.

Harold Horwood's *White Eskimo* is the first novel written about Labrador by a Newfoundlander, and upon its release, it was eagerly purchased not just by Newfoundlanders and Labradorians; it made Canadian national bestseller lists for seventeen weeks in a row and was released in five other countries. Horwood's anti-Christian, anti-capitalist stance made a change from the sentimental adventures of the earlier Grenfellian works of fiction, but whether the change was for the better was and is a matter of debate.

The plot is not complicated. A white giant of a man arrives in Labrador from somewhere in the west, and in a matter of days, he establishes himself as a cult figure who will lead the local Inuit away from the bonds of colonial servitude by setting an example of how people can still live the way they did before the white man came. He dresses in white, has white dogs, and even his komatik is white, so that he is virtually invisible in the snow and ice. The resident religious and medical missionaries, and to some extent the justice system, set out to break his hold on their previously obedient community members, ultimately destroying him and his happy family.

Horwood employs a preface, unusual in a novel, to establish his credentials, claiming he had "traveled in Labrador extensively for many years before undertaking this book," and later "after a considerable absence" was able to refamiliarize himself with the place. Having no inconsiderable familiarity with the north myself, as well as twelve years' residence in Labrador, I think I am as qualified to judge the accuracy of what he wrote as he was to write it in the first place.

Horwood is the first one to admit the characters in *White Eskimo* are based on real people. First there is the Moravian missionary, Manfred Kosh, modelled on Paul Hettasch, a long-time resident of Nain; next is Hugh Richardson, who bears a striking resemblance to the trader Richard White; then there is the policeman Julius Finnan, who walked this earth under the name Frank Mercer from Bay Roberts; and finally, we have Dr. Tocsin, a thoroughly Grenfellian medical man. The central character, a rogue trapper-trader known as Esau Gillingham or the White Spirit, appears as himself, though I'm not sure that his relatives in Gander Bay would have recognized him as he appears in the pages of this book.

The first thing a reader is likely to notice about

the book is that it is built on stereotypes. All the missionaries are greedy, indolent and dishonest, the traders are avaricious but redeemable, and as a rule all the non-Inuit we encounter in these pages are thoroughly untrustworthy types. The Inuit, on the other hand, are childlike, honest, hard-working, downtrodden folk whose only fault is to have allowed outsiders to dictate how they should live. Readers will have no trouble separating the villains from the heroes in the course of this novel.

The story unwinds on the *Kyle*, a ship that served as the Labrador coastal boat from 1926 to 1959. The events that culminated in Gillingham being accused of murdering Abel Shiwak (a fictional surrogate for Mark Kennitok) took place around 1936. Gathered on the *Kyle* are a number of traders, the policeman, an omniscient narrator, and as we discover on the last page, the author himself. There are a few Inuit women present, but as Horwood writes them, they have nothing to add to the story, so we hardly notice them. Tracking who is speaking at any given point is tricky, sometimes hinted at by a change in the typeface of the text, but it doesn't really matter, as all the voices sound much the same.

The first hint that Horwood may have overreached himself comes on the first page, where he describes the men prosecuting the Labrador fishery during the summer months as "nomads." In my dictionary, nomads are wanderers, people who roam from place to place. The crews that traditionally pursued fish on the Labrador came from Conception Bay and other areas of Newfoundland, as well as New England and elsewhere. They were "stationers," setting up rough fishing rooms for seasonal use. These stationers had permanent homes they went back to, and whenever possible they had shacks or cabins in specific harbours and coves in Labrador that they returned to year after year. It's a small point, but it's the first of a lot of small points that undermine this reader's capacity for suspending disbelief.

Are large dogs more efficient than smaller huskies? Horwood would get an argument about that from the mushers I know. Had beaver been so trapped out in Labrador by the time of this novel that "No one had seen a beaver in Labrador for some four or five generations"? Beavers were certainly in short supply in Labrador during the years in which this novel is set, but to claim that beaver had been wiped out for about 100 years is simply not plausible.

Horwood also refers to the traders as giving the Inuit the benefit of "the cash income of trapping." I first went to the Arctic in 1972, the year this book was released, and even then, cash was hard to come by. Almost everything went on tick at the store, and if you happened to pay cash when they were short of change, you got the balance in bubble gum, which the kids hanging around outside the store were happy to relieve you of. In their trip over the Kiglapaits, Horwood has Gillingham and the policeman stop to "make tea and have a mug-up, a habit Gillingham had picked up from the Eskimos." Does he really think that a Gander Bay man had to learn this from

Inuit? And Inuit don't burp to compliment a good meal—anthropologists say Europeans tend to endow all unfamiliar peoples with this Chinese practice. I'd bet my life that Horwood never experienced this burping custom. I certainly haven't.

There are long passages throughout the book describing travel by boat and on foot, hunting trips, tending traplines, watching the northern lights and spotting exotic animals, and although most of my experience of these things occurred much further north than Labrador, nothing unlikely or inaccurate stood out in Horwood's lavish descriptions. Maybe the animals were a bit thicker on the fictional ground than in reality, but the lemmings and bears and lynx are there, and you do get to see them every now and again if you travel with Innu or Inuit.

However, Horwood seems to have reserved his not inconsiderable gift of description for the environment and the natural world. All the empathy and insight he exhibits in these passages, he fails to display in his descriptions of humans.

Horwood's limited view of missionaries and traders becomes even narrower when he depicts Inuit. His Inuit are gullible, cheerful, soft spoken, easily satisfied, and limited. The most specific he gets is to assure the reader that "Any Eskimo can pick a lock with his eyes shut." His depiction of Inuit women is even more restricted; Inuit women are subservient to men, particularly their husbands; they are quiet, silent, obedient, sexually accessible even at a very young age, and "start to collapse into middle age the day they get a husband." In Horwood's depiction, Inuit women display not an ounce of individual personality. Obviously Horwood never met any of the hundreds of Inuit women I have known over the last fifty years, because in my experience, they are as varied and different from one another as women anywhere in the world.

How the real historic figures compare to the fictional versions Horwood created has interested the critics over the years. Paul Hettasch, on whom the character Manfred Kosh was based, was not living alone in a twenty-room fort; he lived in the mission house with his wife and daughter and several helpers. William Peacock writes in *Reflections from a Snowhouse* that Hettasch did not deserve the "cruel caricature of the missionary villain" portrayed by Horwood. While Kosh might have been appalled at Esau Gillingham selling beer to the Inuit, Hettasch would have known that in earlier times, the Moravians often paid their workers with beer.

Policeman Julius Finnan, a.k.a. Frank Mercer, is redeemed when he quits the police and becomes a civil servant. The real Mercer, in John Parsons' book *Probably Without Equal*, is said to have taken some pride in having been the only law enforcement officer to have served in the Newfoundland Rangers, the Newfoundland Constabulary, and the Royal Canadian Mounted Police. He died at home in Bay Roberts in 2005 at the ripe old age of 91.

Richard White, who appears in the novel as independent trader Hugh Richardson, was, if anything, quirkier than Horwood makes him. From a prominent St. John's merchant family, White studied law at the London School of Economics, went off to the Yukon gold rush, ended up as a trader in Nain where he went head-to-head with the Moravian traders, married two Inuit sisters (though not at the same time), served in the Canadian Expeditionary Force in Russia, and fathered a large family. His youngest child, Winston, became a well-known CBC reporter.

Dr. Tocsin, Kosh's partner in evil, bears an uncanny resemblance to Sir Wilfred Grenfell. Both were notoriously bad navigators who loved to be photographed at the wheel of a ship, but for all their faults, it is unlikely that Grenfell or the Moravian Missions made a fortune exploiting the Inuit. Horwood claimed that the Tocsin/Grenfell craft program sold the product of the Labradorians' hard work "at a thousand percent profit or more," while the Moravians "grew wealthy on trade with the Inuit," when they bought furs from the natives "for a tenth of their value and shipped to Europe at a thousand percent profit." This is hyperbole, not mathematics. Yes, they both made money on their dealing with locals, but that money and a good deal more went back into programs, however ill-conceived, for the communities they served.

Esau Gillingham, as recorded in Gary Saunders's *Rattles and Steadies*, was "the love child of an unmarried Gillingham girl in Gander Bay." Saunders's father Brett, a relative of Gillingham, told him that Gillingham was not a giant, but rather was "thick-set and of average height with bushy eyebrows and a big black beard." In Labrador, he was anything but a revered cult figure. Saunders says "he was not well liked by the people there," and they "called him a name that meant 'Bad Man.'" He sold moonshine, and in Okak Bay he was thought to have shot his partner while coming out of the bush with the winter's furs. Gillingham claimed the man drowned coming through the rapids, and when they recovered the body, it was so decomposed that no bullet wound could be seen.

Gillingham himself neither drowned nor broke his back falling off a fish flake, as some writers have reported. Brett Saunders said that his body was found on the beach near Jack's Feeder on Gander Lake. "It seems that he was getting ready to cook his supper when he felt the need to relieve himself and that while taking down his pants he suffered a fatal heart attack or a stroke." The crows had picked out both his eyes—not exactly a romantic end for a back-to-the-land cult hero.

There is another, less literary source of information on Esau Gillingham, and that's the legend of Old Smoker, who has also been known as the White Eskimo. Smoker, like Gillingham, was said to dress in white, drive a team of white dogs and a white komatik, and was known throughout the region, ready to lead lost travellers to safety. Once a traveller was safe, Smoker disappeared, leaving no track or trace of his komatik or team.

Accounts of the appearance of Smoker come

from every part of Labrador and even the Great Northern Peninsula of Newfoundland. John C. Kennedy suggests that the legend of Old Smoker "resembles Stith Thompson's motif of a person transformed," like the devil who disappears in a puff of smoke. The story of Old Smoker greatly resembles a well-known American legend about a cowboy who "has a vision of red-eyed, steel-hooved cattle... being chased by the spirits of damned cowboys." Lyricist Stan Jones heard the story when he was a boy, and in 1948 he composed the famous song "Ghost Riders in the Sky," which was still popular throughout my childhood. Smoker has more recently morphed into the motorcyclist Johnny Blade, a spectral stunt man played by Nicholas Cage in the film *Ghost Rider*. Some Labradorians, including John O. Heard in his ballad "The Wreck of the Two-Five-O," claim that Smoker has now got a snowmobile.

Old Smoker probably predates Gillingham's 1930s arrival in Labrador, where he set up as a trapper but got into trouble for breaches of the game and liquor laws, selling moonshine, or 'smoke' as it was known, to the local Inuit. He is thought to have reformed on his deathbed, promising to lead the lost to safety to make up for his sins. The deathbed redemption would explain why a fox-poisoner, bootlegger, and possible murderer might become a helpful ghost, but it does not really explain why Esau Gillingham inherited his name and reputation.

Readers are left with the question of why, if *White Eskimo* was so flawed, it was so popular with people across Canada. Probably because it conforms to the stereotypes already held by the general public—that of the untrustworthy, violent, male "Indian" and the peaceful, gentle, female "Eskimo" posited by Margaret Atwood in her book *Survival*, published in the same year as *White Eskimo*. Does it matter whether a character or plot is drawn from life? Not as long as the novel tells a compelling story. *White Eskimo* would not convince someone who is familiar with the Inuit north, but it probably would convince a reader who knew no Inuit.

One question remains, which neither Horwood nor the many others who have written about the White Eskimo have settled—did Gillingham murder either Mark Kennitok or Kennitok's fictional doppelganger, Abel Shiwak? It's not clear whether there was a murder at all. Neither the historic nor the fictional Esau Gillingham was ever convicted of the death. According to Addison Brown, in reality, the post mortem was conducted by Dr. Lionel Forsythe of the International Grenfell Association, the result being a finding of "death by a fall and not a blow administered by another." In Horwood's novel, the body is brought to Cartwright, where an autopsy performed by Drs. Tocsin and McTag find that Abel died from "a wound consistent with that of a bullet fired from a small-bore, high-velocity rifle," but no parts of the bullet were recovered. Nevertheless, both the real and the fictional cases were sent to the grand jury, where they were dismissed.

This is where the boundary between historical

fiction and fact must be drawn. Horwood's narrator explains that the defence "often makes no statement at all before the Grand Jury." In this case, however, the defence argued that there had been no valid autopsy, because the relevant document was signed only by Dr. Tocsin, and not co-signed by Dr. McTag. The fictional Gillingham was released, and a month later tried on a minor breach of the liquor laws. According to Brett Saunders, the real Gillingham was charged only with liquor offenses after an autopsy in Cartwright revealed that Abel had been killed by a blow to the back of the head, not a bullet.

Horwood, a seasoned journalist, must surely have been aware that while the Crown attorney presented evidence at a grand jury hearing, neither defence counsel nor the accused were, in practice, permitted to attend grand jury proceedings. The result in both real and fictional cases was the same, so why Horwood chose to fudge the functioning of the grand jury is a mystery. If it had not been for Horwood's insistence on the historic roots of his tale, such a major inconsistency with historic fact might have been ignored. The only answer I can come up with is that both reality and fiction serve Harold Horwood's personal agenda—to condemn colonial domination by government, church, and mercantile interests, and to exalt the back-to-the-land movement.

*

Considering that all these books are set in Labrador, there is remarkably little about Labrador in most of them. Instead, Labrador simply functions as a remote, little-known location in which to set a series of improbable adventures of the sort boys would find appealing. Today, with native-born Labradorians such as Alex Saunders, Dorothy Mesher, George Rich, Elizabeth Penashue, George Gregoire, Anne Budgell, Nikashant Antane, and others producing books, young readers can hope that novels with authentic Labrador settings will soon be available. And if they aren't, then perhaps those young readers will write their own, in time to come.

Morgen Mills, writing in *Newfoundland and Labrador Studies*, has pointed out that "fiction is not a significant component of Labrador literature." Even a superficial survey of books about Labrador confirms that while non-fiction such as memoirs and autobiographies focusing on Labrador are appearing regularly on publishers' lists, there is a dearth of novels about Labrador, and those that do exist have virtually all been written by people from outside.

Both the First and the Second World Wars had to be endured and survived before any author broke the mould of Boy's Own adventure tales to offer a somewhat different take on Labrador. By this time, quite a few military people had acquired at least a passing acquaintance with the air base at Goose Bay and its various military outposts at Makkovik and elsewhere. Not surprisingly, air travel featured in many of these works.

Nevil Shute was already a best-selling author when he published *No Highway* in 1948, a novel about a plane crash in Labrador. In brief, the plot revolves around an eccentric airplane designer, Theodore Honey, who suspects that metal fatigue has caused the plane to crash. On his way out to Labrador to look into the matter, Honey realizes that the plane he is flying on is of the same type, so he sabotages the craft on the tarmac in Gander to prevent it flying, thus saving the lives of the passengers and crew.

There really isn't much about Labrador in this book, but you do get a lovely snapshot of Gander airport. The novel was made into a film in 1951, with Jimmy Stewart as a stuttering Honey and Marlene Dietrich as an aging movie star. Shute, an aviation engineer and designer himself, almost certainly had first-hand knowledge of Labrador.

Published originally in 1955, John Wyndham's science fiction novel *The Chrysalids* is set in a post-nuclear-holocaust, climate-changed Labrador that at first seems totally unfamiliar. Living in one of the few places in the world to remain relatively intact, Labradorians in the novel have turned away from mining and lumbering to become farmers. The land, however, is plagued with mutant plants, animals, and people, all of which are deemed abominations and destroyed in an attempt to retain the true image of God as described in the Bible.

Into this struggling agrarian society are born a number of children who on the outside appear to be normal, but who can communicate with one another by telepathy. As they grow up, the children realize that if their difference is detected, they will be hunted down, sterilized, and driven into the mutated wilderness which surrounds their home farms. Politically, *The Chrysalids* can be read as Wyndham's take on the Nazi racial purges and eugenics programs of the 1940s, as well as an anti-nuclear plea for disarmament, a theme also expanded in Shute's *On the Beach*, which was later made into a film with Gregory Peck and Ava Gardner.

In the 1960s, *The Chrysalids* became a cult classic, with huge sales. The lyrics for the Jefferson Airplane hit song "Crown of Creation" are derived directly from the closing chapters of the book, and the last verse of Neil Young's "After the Gold Rush" describes the ending of the book, when telepaths from another surviving group arrive to rescue the children. Penguin reissued the work, replacing the original cover of a single six-toed child's footprint with a colourful image of a green-skinned, lobster-clawed alien with medieval armour and a parka.

The novel had its critics, but it is, without argument, a very readable and compelling story, though you have to search carefully for its setting's resemblance to Labrador. The communities are small and isolated, there is a strong reliance on oral tradition, the population is highly religious and informally ruled by Elders' groups such as were once found in Nain or Hopedale, and the environment is both generous and dangerous. Beneath the book's superficial details, *The Chrysalids* comes nearer than some more realistic novels to reflecting the actual daily lives of Labrador children in the 1950s.

Williwaw, by Phyllis S. Moore, appeared in 1978 and probably created a bit of a stir. The book opens with Labrador about to achieve independence from Canada through peaceful means. Then a Quebec separatist army invades, intent upon "taking back" what they consider rightfully theirs and using the coup to further their own nationalistic aims.

Williwaw has its quota of sentiment and romantic love, but it is also is full of characters who express racist and outdated, politically incorrect attitudes, and the love affair is saddled with a particularly brutal rape and some vivid descriptions of murders. The violence and the bigotry depicted in the book offended many who felt it was insulting to real Labradorians. However, the resentment many Labradorians felt towards their colonial masters in St. John's and Ottawa in the 70s is convincingly real. Some still feel that resentment today, particularly with respect to the Muskrat Falls development.

The Afterlife of George Cartwright, poet John Steffler's debut novel, appeared in 1992 and was surely the first truly successful work of fiction about Labrador. Based on Captain George Cartwright's Labrador journals, it has plenty of outdoor adventure and the obligatory minor love story, but Cartwright is a ghost who is condemned to spend 170 years reliving the last day of his life, out on his horse hunting with his hawk and remembering Labrador and its people.

Afterlife's success is derived from its complex characterization, the author's awareness that the reader knows more or less what happened to Cartwright and the Inuit he travelled with, the dual nature of the narration, and above all the exploration of the motivations of the people involved. There is also a surprising and satisfying ending. *Afterlife* was a breakthrough in terms of Labrador fiction for not being a potboiler, but a literary work that will stand the test of time.

Katherine Govier's *Creation*, which was released in 2002, was the author's seventh novel, a book worth waiting for. Like Steffler, Govier anchored her work in solid archival research when she took on the life and work of John James Audubon, the great bird artist, who visited Labrador in the summer of 1833. Most of Audubon's life is well documented, by himself and others, with the exception of those months in Labrador, and it is this blank that Govier tries to fill with plausible fiction.

There are two main threads to the plot: Audubon's revelations about himself (dubious parentage, debts, lack of scientific training), and his growing awareness that his love of birds is as fatal to them as is his love for his family and friends. In essence, this is a novel about ecological destruction which uses Labrador's extinct auks, ducks, and curlews as a cautionary tale. Govier also manages to capture the rather stark beauty of the fogbound Strait of Belle Isle in a way that most Labradorians would recognize, in part because she sticks to effectively vague generalizations.

Kathleen Winter's *Annabel*, published in 2010, was shortlisted for almost every major literary prize it qualified for, but it won none of them, possibly because readers suspected that at heart, its setting and characters just weren't convincing. *Annabel* tells the story of a child born with both a penis and a vagina, in a Labrador village that strongly resembles North West River. The parents and the midwife keep the child's dual sex a secret, and as the father wants a son, the baby is raised as a boy named Wayne. The midwife, who isn't convinced this is the best route to go, calls Wayne's alternate nature Annabel, after her dead daughter.

The plot follows Wayne's development as an intersex child in a hyper-masculine hunting society, until as an adolescent he chooses to stop taking male hormones. Wayne/Annabel doesn't transition to a female gender identity, but embraces neither and both male and female genders. Child and parents alike struggle to navigate the challenges of coming to terms with a unique and complex relationship to gender and social roles.

Readers elsewhere were charmed by the lyrical passages describing the place, the people, and Wayne/Annabel's understanding of the world, but readers in Labrador were repeatedly ambushed by errors large and small. Natural history is altered, family names are misappropriated, and roads and bridges appear or disappear at will. In fact, it became something of a game for Labrador readers to outdo one another in identifying the hundreds of errors they found in *Annabel*. And what Winter knows about intersex people, you could fit in your eye.

There are other novels about Labrador, including those by Dillon Wallace, the *Bob Morane* series in French by Belgian Henri Vernes, *Labrador* by Kathryn Davis, and for killer bees and "oodles of gay sex," as *Quill and Quire* put it, *The Lava in My Bones* by Barry Webster. *Chronoreg*, by Daniel Sernine, picks up where P.S. Moore's *Williwaw* left off, but with an added science fiction twist. It's curious how many of the recent books explore the impact of sexual non-conformity in a highly controlled and puritanical society.

It's pretty clear from this brief summary of what's out there for Labrador's adult readers that they will have to wait until there are more Labrador fiction writers to get anything they can comfortably sink their teeth into. In the meantime, there are three good novels about Labrador that are worth reading, and lots of good home-grown non-fiction to fill those long winter evenings.

Profiles and Biographies

Kenn Harper; Len Rich; Dorrie Brown; Anne Budgell; Nikashant Antane; Emma Anderson; Eldon Drodge; Mark Kurlansky

March 2014

I generally bring a good dose of skepticism to works about Inuit and the Arctic, but Kenn Harper always delivers the genuine goods, as he does with *In Those Days: Inuit Lives*. You can be sure that any work with his name on it is thoroughly researched, carefully composed, and triple-checked for errors. A fluent Inuktitut speaker, Harper has spent his entire adult life tracking down obscure facts, exposing falsities, and delighting in the complexity of a culture so unlike the one he was born into.

In Those Days is a collection of profiles of Inuit from across the circumpolar world, many of them with Newfoundland and Labrador connections. Rather than biographies, which document full lives, profiles are outline or short character sketches, giving a taste of what their subjects are or were like, and often focusing not on rounded characters, but rather on some specific aspect of people's lives. The Labradorians of *In Those Days* include Mikak, who helped found the Moravian church in this part of the world; Simon Gibbons, from Forteau, who became the first Inuk to be ordained a minister; and John Shiwak, the Inuk sniper who died at the Battle of Cambrai in 1917.

Harper also includes profiles of the Labrador Inuit who went to the Chicago World's Fair in 1893. Foremost of these is Nancy Columbia, who was born at the fair and grew up to be a movie star, and poor little "Prince" Pomiuk, who was crippled in a fall there and later became one of Grenfell's chief means of raising money for the hospital at Battle Harbour.

Kallihirua, also called Erasmus York, wasn't a Labradorian but a Greenlander. He went to Newfoundland via England in 1854 to study theology prior to setting off on a mission to Labrador with the Anglican Bishop. Sadly, he caught a chill and died in St. John's the following summer. His grave is in the cemetery of the Anglican Cathedral on Duckworth Street, opposite the Courthouse.

Greenlanders Taqulittuq and Ebierbing, called Hannah and Joe in English, were more fortunate. Shipwrecked on an ice floe off the coast of Greenland, they and their companions drifted in the North Atlantic for six months, covering 1,500 miles. After terrible privation, they were rescued by Captain Isaac Bartlett and the men of the sealing vessel *Tigress*.

Another of Harper's profiles is of Makpi, who as a child survived the wreck of the *Karluk*. She was just two years old when Bob Bartlett and the Inuk hunter Kataktovik left her and the rest of their party at

Wrangel Island and made their epic journey across to Siberia. It was six months before the captain was able to find a ship to rescue them. The photo of Makpi on the cover of Harper's book was taken in Nome, Alaska, after Bartlett and Kataktovik returned, and there's not a feather out of her. She lived to be 97.

All the profiles of Inuit in this collection are interesting, and the illustrations Harper has collected are first-rate.

In Those Days, listed as "Book 1," is now a series of five books: 1. *Inuit Lives*; 2. *Arctic Crime and Punishment*; 3. *Tales of Arctic Whaling*; 4. *Shamans, Spirits, and Faith in the Inuit North*; and 5. *Inuit and Explorers*.

May 2009

Although *Bill Bennett: Pioneer Bush Pilot and Outfitter*, by the late Len Rich, advertises itself as a biography, it is really just a collection of anecdotes about two specific aspects of Bennett's life: fishing and flying. Rich writes that Bennett's "personal life . . . is not mentioned, because that is not what this book is about," but even bush pilots don't exist in a vacuum. There is no organized outline of his business life here either. What this brief little book does do is give profiles of the guides, family, and friends Bill Bennett worked with. It is really a book aimed at Bennett's inner circle, not at the general public.

Like anyone who has spent a lot of time in the north, I've witnessed the power and the glory of the bush pilot, and I have a few war stories of my own to tell, but anecdotes do not make a good book, and they certainly don't constitute a biography. If you knew Bill Bennett, this book will probably trigger fond memories, but it isn't really enlightening for someone who didn't know him, and it doesn't add much to the documentation of the outfitting industry or even to aviation history in the province.

March 2010

Uncommon Clay: The Labradoria Mural by Dorrie Brown is really more of an art book, but since it gives literal and literary snapshots of almost five dozen young Labradorians, caught in a narrow span of time, it could also be considered a series of profiles. In November 2006, the Labrador Creative Arts Festival brought in an art educator from British Columbia to work with students on clay tiles depicting images from their communities. The clay needed for the tiles had to be transported in a heated truck, and organizers discovered that it was cheaper to bring in four times as much clay as they needed. The tile workshops went so well that local educator Dorrie Brown, who had been learning the techniques alongside the students, decided to expand the project to produce a full-scale mural suitable for the anticipated new theatre that Danny Williams had promised the community.

Four years and a lot of hard work later, the mural was officially opened at the Lawrence O'Brien Arts Centre. It comprises fifty-four large clay tiles by students from thirteen communities depicting images from the Innu, Inuit, NunatuKavummiut, and Livyer traditions. The total cost was $33,000, most of which came from corporate donors and government grants. Many of the originating artists were on hand for the opening, along with a yaffle of VIPs, and everyone agreed that it was well worth the work, the cost, and the long wait.

Uncommon Clay, a record of the development and realization of the Labradoria mural, was launched at the official opening of the mural, and it is a gorgeous work. Each of the tiles is given a two-page spread with a full-page reproduction of the tile and a page dedicated to the young artist who produced it, which includes photos of the student and an artist's statement about the image and the experience of producing it.

First, the tiles themselves are stunning. In some cases the individual images are clumsy or predictable, while in others they are surprisingly sophisticated and clever, but the overall effect is marvelous. The unity of the mural has been guaranteed by a complex process of triple painting the fired tiles, which produces a consistent antiqued effect of bronze, copper, silver, and gold tones. Animals, people, buildings, and landscapes all come together in an impressive montage, and it is only on closer inspection that you realize that the mural includes such disparate elements as an Innu protester urinating on a police car and a pair of moose eating water weeds for lunch.

Although clay tile work may seem foreign to the Labrador tradition, a close reading of the introduction reveals that the patterns were transferred to clay using the old method used for hooked mats—a pin and a piece of paper. The bas relief process is also not unlike caribou or moose hair tufting, a technique that is attracting renewed interest in the Goose Bay area.

The photos of the students are equally diverse, and almost as interesting as the tiles themselves. The young people are posed in a variety of ways—an athlete carrying the Olympic torch, Miss Teen Canada perched on a dogsled with a tiara on her head, a young girl driving a snowmobile in her shirtsleeves, a boy slumped in an armchair reading a book. Often there are two photos: one of the student working on the tile or holding the unfired clay, and another, taken later, with or without the finished piece. These photos make you realize how young some of these children were, and how they were growing into adults as the mural process progressed.

The accompanying artists' statements, some of which are translated to or from Labrador Inuttitut and Innu-aimun, are revealing. Many of the students seemed to find the challenge of working in a new medium stressful, and they lacked confidence at first. However, the satisfaction they express upon seeing the completed tile suggests that maybe our youth need more stressful challenges, rather than fewer. The kids were inspired by a variety of people, and they mention teachers, deceased grandparents, and relatives other than their parents, a reminder that the extended family and community still matter to our young people.

December 2013

Retired CBC reporter Anne Budgell has the heart of a novelist. *Dear Everybody: A Woman's Journey from Park Avenue to a Labrador Trapline* is a biography of Barbara Mundy Groves during her years in Labrador, but it has the structure and tension of a work of fiction. It's a terrific read. Groves was a New York socialite who came to work as a volunteer without pay (WOP) with the Industrial Department of the Grenfell Mission at St. Anthony. She was a tall, gangly, rather goofy-looking woman, and when her engagement to a man at home ended badly, she seems to have despaired of ever getting married. She returned to Labrador as a volunteer with the Mission during the Second World War, landing in North West River just when the Goose Bay air base was at its most active.

Barbara Mundy was a bit long in the tooth when she arrived in Labrador, but given that there were up to ten thousand men in Goose Bay and very few women, the obvious direction of this story should have been marriage to a lonely American serviceman. Instead, she fell hard for Labrador and for widowed trapper Russell Groves. Barbara was so taken with the country and the man that she went trapping with him to the Height of Land.

Budgell's gifts here are her insider's knowledge of the place and the people, and her flair for the dramatic. She introduces Groves in the early weeks of her marriage, bewildered and miserable, trying to figure out what is expected of her and not succeeding. The narrative then shifts back to her New York days, before progressing through the stages of her work and her love affair until we catch up with her on the river and learn how both spouses have adjusted to matrimony. Groves left behind several thousand pages of letters, diaries, and notes, but Budgell's background information and research are the glue that binds the story seamlessly together. At over 300 pages, this isn't a short book, but I got so caught up in the life of this warm and charmingly real socialite that I wished it was longer. Spoiler alert: the rather unlikely union lasted for fifty years.

May 2011

Imagine Christian, the hero of *Pilgrim's Progress*, slogging through a frozen Slough of Despond, hauling his burden on a toboggan towards the Celestial City, and you have the gist of *Giant's Dream: A Healing Journey through Nitassinan* by Nikashant Antane, a book which chronicles Michel Andrew's highly publicized walk from Sheshatshiu to Natuashish, through some 400 kilometres of wilderness.

Michel Andrew, known as "The Giant" in his home community of Sheshatshiu, was one of the troubled young Innu caught in the revolving door of the justice system, a suicidal substance-abuser who was seriously at risk. Out on the land, he was hard-working and a capable hunter, a quiet, inarticulate, overgrown boy, strong but soft from too much beer and junk food, too many nights sofa-surfing around the community. He had a reputation for being reliable in the country, but he was a loose cannon in town.

Along came a redemptive woman, a desire to turn his life around, and a decision to walk from Sheshatshiu to Natuashish as his ancestors had done, to show that he could make a plan and stick to it. The Giant was in some ways tailor-made for television: tall, well-proportioned, and ruggedly good-looking. In other ways he was a promoter's nightmare: shy, inarticulate, ill-educated, and uninterested in politics. What followed was a modern story of internet fame and media attention.

Giant's Dream was written by Michel Andrew's uncle, who knows his family history well and is able to project his own memories onto his nephew. He goes back over the recent past to the flooding of the Upper Churchill and the low-level flying protests of the 1980s, putting Giant's unhappy childhood into a historic context.

The photographs, of which there are dozens, are given lots of space. For the most part, they present public faces: Giant embracing friends and relatives at the start and finish of his walk, groups posing together, individuals looking straight at the camera. However, for people unfamiliar with the Innu, these images provide a way to see into the community, while still protecting Innu privacy. One particular photo, of seventeen young people in white Innu hunting clothes, marching in a line with their toboggans towards the camera, elicited the phrase "an Innu army!" from several people I showed it to. Indeed, if you could enlist that army in the cause of Innu health and sobriety, the war would be easily won.

So far, this story has a happy continuation, which is better than a happy ending. Giant raised $26,000 for the dialysis unit at Happy Valley-Goose Bay with his first walk, and in the subsequent two years has led many more young people on wilderness walks down into Quebec. The love story didn't quite work out, but he survived the break-up without coming apart, and he seems to have found the direction he was looking for. The Giant, Michel Andrew, may yet present the world with an army of foot soldiers for health.

*

August 2009

Betrayal of Faith: The Tragic Journey of a Colonial Native Convert, by Emma Anderson, tells the story of an eleven-year-old Indigenous boy named Pastedechouan who in 1620 was taken to be educated in France by the Recollet order of the Catholic Church. Four years later, he returned to the St. Lawrence, first to Quebec City where he lived at the Recollet headquarters, and then back to Tadoussac, where his people lived in summertime. Not long after, the English successfully laid siege to Quebec, the Recollet fathers were deported, and as Anderson puts it, Pastedechouan was "compelled to seek succor and alliance with the people he had been taught to regard as his religious and cultural inferiors."

Pastedechouan was Innu, one of the people who regularly traveled and hunted over the then nonexistent Quebec-Labrador border, the same group who eventually settled in Sheshatshiu. The connection between Pastedechouan and the present-day people of Sheshatshiu is more than an interesting coincidence, for what happened to Pastedechouan precedes and informs the history of Indigenous residential schools in Canada and sheds light on the politics and activism today. *Betrayal of Faith* documents historic injustices and trauma that even today haunt the Indigenous community in Labrador and elsewhere in Canada.

Prior to the officially sanctioned Christianization of the Innu of the St. Lawrence River area, Innu-European relations were almost entirely economic and military. As Emma Anderson explains it, such relations were mutually beneficial. Once the Catholic Church got into the mix, however, things changed. Traders were willing and anxious to take Innu to Europe for training as interpreters or exhibition as exotics, while Innu saw these visits as a means to forge military alliances and learn about trade partners. Innu returning from Europe brought home information and skills which gave them an edge in the competitive fur trade. Therefore, when the French priests asked for Innu children to send to France for their education, the Innu anticipated that on their return, these children would improve Innu trade and war tactics, and willingly handed over their sons.

The Recollet strategy was to isolate children from their relatives, convert them to the tenets of Catholicism, and then reeducate them to view their families and their entire culture as backward, savage, and loathsome. The Innu sent their sons out to France expecting to receive them back as ambassador-spies, but instead, what they got back were brainwashed children in men's bodies.

Upon his return, Pastedechouan knew nothing of French commercial life and had not been initiated into Innu adult life—and did not wish to be. He was incapable of hunting and even claimed he had forgotten how to speak Innu-aimun. At seventeen, he had nothing to offer except the dubious spiritual insights of the Recollet order and an unshakeable belief in the superiority of French society. By the time the English had expelled his Recollet mentors, Pastedechouan was regarded by his family as an "idiot," a "blockhead," and a "know-nothing," "physically adult but religiously and culturally still a child." Because success in hunting was tied to Innu religious belief, Pastedechouan was entirely dependent upon his three older brothers for everything. He was not even useful in negotiating trade, as he was defiantly loyal to the French whose economic policies were so at odds with the well-being of the Innu.

By 1632, when the Jesuit mission was reestablished at Quebec, Pastedechouan had refamiliarized himself enough with the Innu language to obtain work with the colonial government as a translator, and for the next four years he was a language tutor to Father Paul Le Jeune. Theirs was a love-hate relationship that ended when, following the deaths of his three brothers, Pastedechouan died of starvation and exposure in the winter of 1636.

There are at least two important lessons to be learned from Anderson's academic analysis of the betrayal of Pastedechouan. First, she uses all the historic and anthropological resources at her disposal to outline the traditional Innu method of child-rearing. She gives us a sense of what Pastedechouan's education would have been like prior to his conversion. In my experience, Innu children are raised in a similar manner today, at least until they begin attending school, and the method works. On trips into the bush, I have seen even the smallest toddlers soldier on without complaint in a way that would put to shame a veteran of a hundred forced marches.

Secondly, Anderson outlines clearly how teaching Innu children to reject, ridicule and reform traditional Innu values results in immaturity, dependence, and despondency. Not surprisingly, in today's society this self-loathing can lead to substance abuse and suicide. More surprisingly, four hundred years of failure has not discouraged non-Innu from trying to reeducate Innu children, much as Pastidechouan was reeducated.

In 2009, Innu in Labrador took control of their own schools. It will be interesting to see whether the government is willing to give them four centuries to reverse the trend. When *akenashau* educators grow impatient with the pace of Innu success, I hope someone puts a copy of *Betrayal of Faith* into their hands. Despite a few errors in Anderson's summation of more recent Innu history, it is, along with Georg Henriksen's *I Dreamed the Animals*, one of the most important books about the Innu to be published in recent years.

August 2002

Most Newfoundlanders and Labradorians are familiar with the story of William Jackman's heroics at Spotted Island. During the October gale of 1867, a schooner, the *Sea Clipper*, was damaged in a collision with another vessel and subsequently driven on the rocks, where it looked as if all 27 souls on board faced almost certain death. William Jackman from Renews, who happened to see the wreck, swam to the damaged vessel and began carrying crew and passengers to land on his back. With the help of John and Samuel Holwell of Spotted Island, he safely brought all twenty-seven to land.

Eldon Drodge's account of this famous rescue, *Jackman: The Courage of Captain William Jackman*, has a handsome cover and adequately clear photo illustrations, but unfortunately it adopts the conventions of the novel without its freedom of invention. The blurry line between what the author knows and what he made up created problems for me.

We are told all through the book what this or that person thought or felt, and some people, such as the last person Jackman brought off the *Sea Clipper*, are given fictional names, yet the work tried hard not to be fiction. Despite the footnotes, it is impossible for a reader to know what is fact and what isn't. When authors assign fictional names to historic figures, they lose credibility.

I would have been interested to know why none of the reports of Jackman's famous rescue identifies the twenty-seventh passenger he brought off the *Sea Clipper*. She was thought to have been the 41-year-old cook off the *Loon*, from Clarke's Beach, who died of injuries sustained when the *Loon* and the *Sea Clipper* collided. Some accounts say she was pregnant and gave birth that dreadful night, while others claim that she was dying of tuberculosis, yet it was apparently impossible to identify her. Drodge's *Jackman* isn't a badly written book, but it poses more questions than it answers.

June 2012

I read and thoroughly enjoyed Mark Kurlansky's *Cod* and *Salt*, and I was looking forward to *Birdseye: The Adventures of a Curious Man*, his profile of the man who invented—or more accurately, identified—the process of flash freezing food. However, I got positively excited when I read on the first page that Clarence Birdseye had filled eight leather-bound journals during his time in Labrador, including the summer of 1912, when he volunteered to work with Wilfred Grenfell aboard the medical mission ship *Strathcona*.

I rushed though the opening chapters about chasing ticks in the Bitterroot Valley to get to Chapter 5, titled appropriately, "Frozen," but sadly, what I found was a bit disappointing. Don't get me wrong—Kurlansky can write. Even the Montana ticks were interesting, and I learned a great deal about dehydration, electric light bulbs, and a number of other subjects before I turned the last page of *Birdseye*. But given the wealth of material he had to draw on, the Labrador chapters were oddly off the mark.

For starters, Kurlansky relies almost entirely on the various autobiographies by Sir Wilfred Grenfell himself as sources of information on the doctor's career, so a number of prevarications and evasions are left unaddressed. For example, Kurlansky states that "Starting in 1902 he [Grenfell] spent every other winter in Labrador." About the only thing Labradorians agree upon with regard to Grenfell is that the good doctor never passed even one winter in this country, let alone any number of them. In local parlance, Sir Wilfred "said more than his prayers." Kurlansky mentions that Grenfell's yacht *Strathcona* was paid for by Lord Strathcona, who drove the last spike in the Canadian Railway, but he fails to mention that as Donald Smith, Lord Strathcona had been the head trader at North West River for many years, which explained his interest in the health of Labradorians.

Birdseye was a huge fan of Grenfell, and apparently the admiration was returned. It was Grenfell who urged the scientist to experiment with fox farming in Labrador, experiments that eventually led to the development of flash-frozen foods, and Grenfell even raised capital for the venture. Despite their difference in age and religious belief, Birdseye and Grenfell formed a firm friendship that they maintained over the years. Perhaps this mutual loyalty is why details of Birdseye's time in Labrador are so often nudged slightly off track due to some minor error or omission on Kurlansky's part.

The weakness of the Labrador material in *Birdseye* has rather shaken my faith in Kurlansky as a popular historian, but the book is still a good read. My hope is that some budding scholar will come across that reference to Birdseye's eight journals and decide to do a really thorough job of researching his time in Labrador. That's a book I'd really like to read.

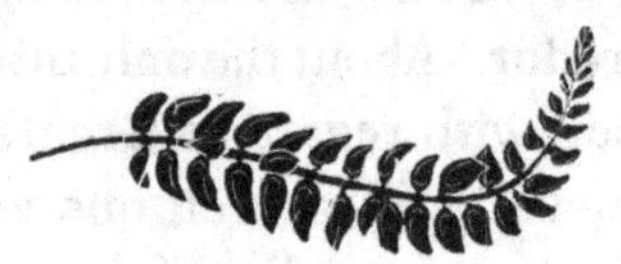

Explorers

Henry Youle Hind; William Hind; Bob Bartlett; Martha MacDonald; Larry Coady

September 2007

WHEN one thinks of early writers about Labrador, George Cartwright immediately comes to mind, but Cartwright saw himself as a settler and businessman, rather than as an explorer. A true explorer travels through a country in order to learn about it. Cartwright's intention was exploitation rather than exploration, though he did both. Among the first explorers who wrote for publication about what they found in Labrador were the brothers Hind. In the summer of 1861, Henry Youle Hind led a party, including his brother William, by canoe up the Moisie River from Sept-Îles to the headwaters near present-day Wabush. Henry Hind's two-volume account of the journey was republished in 2007 by Boulder Press, in a one-volume, paperback edition, including a dozen colour reproductions of William Hind's paintings, as well as numerous etchings and maps, thereby serving to introduce the work of both men.

Explorations in the Interior of the Labrador Peninsula is a massive tome, not the kind of light reading you pack for a day at the beach. However, it is just the kind of book that does well next to the fireplace over a long Labrador winter. It centres on the brothers' canoe trip up the Moisie, but along the way there are numerous stops, side-trips, and diversions to keep the armchair traveler amused.

Henry Hind seems to have been a man of many interests. The Hind brothers were born in Nottingham, England, the sons of an affluent lace manufacturer, and they were given good educations, so that when their father's business failed in the depression of 1837, they were well positioned to come out to the colonies to carve out new lives for themselves. Henry became a professor of Chemistry and Geology at Trinity College, Toronto, and as a fellow of the Royal Geographical Society, he was soon face and eyes into the business of exploration. In 1857 he made an expedition to the Red River Settlement in what is now the province of Manitoba, and the next year another expedition into present-day Saskatchewan. While visiting England to arrange for publication of his book about those expeditions, he expressed an interest in the Labrador.

It is surprisingly difficult to figure out exactly where the Hinds went on their 1861 trip into the interior. Provincial maps of Newfoundland and Labrador show little beyond the provincial border, Quebec maps show everything but the border itself, and the massive changes caused by the Smallwood Reservoir make it hard to match old maps to new. It would seem, however, that nearly all of their journey was in the Quebec part of the peninsula. The truth is, though, that wildlife, rivers, and Indigenous hunters pay little attention to boundaries or maps. This is a story about Labrador, the land and its people.

The Hinds traveled with a number of First Nations and mixed-race guides, so whenever they got bogged down, weathered-in, or otherwise stopped in their progress, there were stories to tell of hunting, fishing, marriages, births, deaths, ghosts, necromancy, avalanches, fires, and floods. In fact, there was almost no subject which was not touched upon at some point in their long arduous journey, so even when Hind had no adventures of his own to report, he had plenty of other people's to record.

Although a remarkably open-minded man, Hind was a product of his time, so certain prejudices inevitably emerge in his accounts of the Innu. For example, when discussing their use of the vapour bath or steam tent for medicinal purposes, he records that, "The conjurers would frequently pretend to see the feeding haunts of the caribou or moose . . . and give the news in a loud voice to the credulous spectators squatting on the outside."

The words "conjurer," "pretend," "credulous," and even "squatting," all serve to undermine the importance Innu attach to envisioning the animal masters, and they say as much about Hind's sense of superiority as they do about the Innu visionaries. Nevertheless, Hind gives us a lot of interesting and important information about Innu life then and now.

Much of *Explorations in the Interior* is taken up

with reports harvested from other writers such as Cartwright, John McLean, the early Jesuits, and other missionaries. Many of the diversions are about areas geographically and culturally far from the Moisie, but they are all presented with energy and enthusiasm. Hind strip-mined the exploration writers of his time, and I can well imagine that he himself is subjected to the same treatment by today's scientists and anthropologists.

Although I took some of Hind's stories with a grain of salt, I confess that I learned a great deal from this book. For instance, Hind explains that there are three kinds of Innu feasts: one at which everything must be eaten, one at which some food is eaten but some must be taken away by the guests, and one at which food may be eaten or left as suits the diners. I have been present at all three kinds of meals with Innu, and I realized there was a pattern, but could not identify it, not even when two elderly Innu women and their interpreter came to my house for Christmas dinner and ended the meal by dividing the remains of the turkey and shoving it into their handbags.

My struggle to find a modern map to assist me in tracing the Hinds' journey was also a useful endeavour. I was reminded that the Labrador boundary is a political invention that is emotionally irrelevant to the Innu of Uashat/Sept-Îles and their relatives in Sheshatshiu and Natuashish.

November 2007

Until I read *Explorations in the Interior,* I had never heard of William Hind and could not have identified anything he had painted. However, upon opening *Defiant Beauty,* the catalogue of an exhibit displayed at The Rooms in 2007, I immediately encountered Hind's portrait of Donald Smith (Lord Strathcona) at North West River, a painting I had seen in reproduction dozens of times.

I had always wondered if that portrait was done in situ or if it had been cobbled together in a studio far from the Labrador wilderness. The buckskin fringes and the bear-claw necklace on the Innu hovering in the background had always seemed a bit Hollywood to me. The three art historians who contributed to *Defiant Beauty* can't answer this question, but they answered a great many others I had, including some that I hadn't even formulated.

Two government surveyors, several French-Canadian voyageurs, and a number of Indigenous guides accompanied the Hind brothers on their 1861 trip. On the way, they encountered more Innu and one, a young Montagnais named Michel, joined them for the remainder of the expedition.

I confess that I was captivated by William's paintings and drawings when I first saw those few that were reproduced in his brother Henry's book. How much more fascinating is the full panoply on display here in the catalogue of all of William Hind's known works from that period. According to Mary Jo Hughes, Henry and William Hind were advancing the tradition of naturalists and explorers such as Sir Joseph Banks, John James Audubon, and Frederick Church. Henry's agenda was to establish the area as a possible route for the North Atlantic Telegraph cable. William's agenda was to assist Henry, and to do that he employed a tool that was almost a trade secret, a camera lucida.

The camera lucida is an optical instrument that allows artists to sketch objects, persons and landscapes quickly and accurately. It is equivalent to the projected photographs that many artists use today, and it allowed for particular accuracy in situations such as map-making and ethnographic illustration. It was a tremendous assistance to Hind in his work, which had to be done quickly while he was being assaulted by flies, smoke, and the weather.

The book's description of the role of the camera lucida in Hind's work is particularly interesting, as it reinforces a sense that Hind was genuinely trying to observe and document without prejudice. The presence in the catalogue of both paintings and later engravings made for publication supports this belief. It was not at all uncommon in previous eras for engravers, with or without the artist's compliance, to alter paintings to make political points.

For example, a watercolour made by Sir John Ross on his 1829-33 expedition to the Arctic shows two Inuit cartographers sketching the west of King

William Island on board his ship *Victory*. An engraving, made for publication from the original, gives the British naval officers much more dignity and changes the scale of the men at the table to suggest a greater distance between the explorers and the Inuit. This parallels discrepancies between Ross's notes and his published account of who was doing the mapping on the voyage, both of which were intended to diminish the explorers' reliance on local knowledge.

William Hind's paintings of the Innu chief Dominique making a map on birch bark illustrates accurately Henry Hind's account of how Dominique's map was essential to the continuation of their journey. Dominique also allowed his son Michel to accompany the expedition as a guide. The sketch of Michel reveals that he was little more than a boy, yet he was trusted by the dozen men to bring them safely to the tablelands. The engraver, probably under William's supervision, adhered strictly to William's delineation.

Having seen some of Labrador's great rivers from canoe and the air, I can testify that Hind's paintings are wonderful realizations of those magnificent landscapes. I can also testify that his portraits of Innu are accurate, as I have seen those faces in their descendants. Every Innu visitor who was over my doorstep in the weeks after I received the book in the mail took the time to pore over the catalogue as if it were a family photo album, which in a way it is.

While the catalogue is a source of joy for many, it also triggers a sense of loss and nostalgia in some Indigenous Labradorians. There have been sighs over the beautiful clothes and artifacts: things we can no longer see in Innu communities. One Elder commented to me on how slim the Innu women were in the paintings, and shook her head over the diabetes which is now epidemic among Innu her age. A young father showed the paintings in the catalogue to his son, pointing out in particular that Innu men had long hair in the old days—the boy had been teased at school over his own beautiful, glossy braids.

I was feeling a certain nostalgia myself in looking at the book, wishing I could swing by The Rooms and see the original paintings. In Labrador, there isn't even a bookstore where people can buy the catalogue.

I'm not sure I will go back very often to Henry Hind's 655-page tome, although the inclusion of an index makes it a useful source of information for future research projects, but I often return to William Hind's illustrations for the sheer pleasure of looking at them and remembering my own explorations of the interior of the peninsula, though I tend to turn the page quickly on the lithograph "Mosquito Lake."

January 2007

Although strictly speaking, Captain Bob Bartlett was a Newfoundlander rather than a Labradorian, no Labrador library would be complete without a few books by and about him. The Bartlett association with Labrador began around 1800, when William "Follow On" Bartlett went looking for seals in Conception Bay in an open boat. Finding no ice, he headed north to Cape Bonavista and the Funks, following on until he was "in the fat" off Hiscock Island in Labrador. Not long after, Follow On's nephew Abram established premises at Turnavik West, an island just north of Makkovik, and set up as a crew captain and supplier until 1884, when he turned the business over to his son William Abram, who by then had almost thirty years of experience in the Labrador fishery.

Although all the Bartlett men and boys wintered from late October to early March in Brigus, Newfoundland, they spent the intervening months in Labrador. Later, when Bob established himself as a freelance explorer and ice navigator, he used Turnavik West as a resupply station on his many voyages in that region, including when he made the infamous trip almost to the North Pole with Admiral Robert Peary.

It's been a hundred years since *The Log of Bob Bartlett* was first published, and fifty since I first read it. My mother, seeing the book in my hands, told me about the time the Captain came to a Christmas party at her parents' house on Long Pond in the

1920s and organized ice pulling competitions with all the dogs in the neighbourhood. That evening, she danced with him at a ball and he trod all over her toes with what she called his "Methodist feet."

Bartlett may not have been much of a dancer, but he was a first-rate storyteller. *The Log of Bob Bartlett* is a quick and entertaining read. Memories of some of his most famous expeditions are interspersed with recollections of his family in Brigus, his views about women, and anecdotes about the people from all walks of life whom he encountered in his long and varied career. Bartlett's publisher, George Palmer Putnam, who was married to Amelia Earhart, was said to have been Bartlett's ghost-writer, and that may be true, but Bartlett could talk, and *The Log* captures at least some of what made me interested in an old explorer who had died before I was even born.

Paul O'Neil wrote in his Foreword to the 2006 reprint that he hoped "to bring the work to the attention of new readers." This is certainly a worthy aim, but I wish he had given at least a hint of the complexities behind the man and his achievements. Despite Bartlett's repeated claims to be a teetotaler, it's no secret that he spent years on skid row in New York, and historian William R. Hunt is clearly skeptical that "Bartlett never used a vulgar word." Also, Bartlett's vigorous defense of Peary's claim to have reached the pole is at odds with the modern consensus that the Admiral fudged his navigation readings. Nevertheless, Bartlett deserved a medal and got one. First published in 1928, *The Log of Bob Bartlett* is very much a product of its time, but even the dust of nearly a century hasn't dimmed the lively, compassionate, witty voice of its author. I'd have risked my toes for a dance with this man any day.

April 2005

The restoration of Hawthorne Cottage in Brigus some years ago prompted a renewed interest in the life and times of Captain Bob Bartlett. There is little dispute over the claim that Bartlett was the greatest ice captain of the twentieth century, but his fame as an explorer has perhaps overshadowed his abilities as a compelling storyteller. Rattling Books, an audiobook company that was based in Tors Cove, Newfoundland, recognized the power of his work and produced a seven-hour recording of probably his best book ever, *The Last Voyage of the Karluk*.

The *Karluk* set out from Vancouver in 1914 to bring a scientific expedition led by Icelandic-Canadian anthropologist Vilhjalmur Stefansson to Herschel Island in the Beaufort Sea. Accompanied by two smaller ships, the *Karluk* headed north, dropping Stefansson along the way, and fought through the ice to within a hundred miles of Herschel. By this time, the two smaller ships had given up and gone into port in Alaska, discharging their scientists to proceed by sledge, but it was too late for the *Karluk*. Bartlett, along with the crew and remnants of the scientific team, were swept back to the westward where the ship was trapped and crushed in the ice.

Bartlett used the little time he had to organize a safe retreat to either Herald or Wrangel Island, and once he had done all he could to secure the lives of his people, he set out with an Inuk companion, Kataktovik, to walk 700 miles over the sea ice to Siberia where he organized a rescue. Four of the scientific party had previously taken their share of the supplies and gone off against Bartlett's advice to find their own way to land. They died, as did four others. The rest owed their lives to the tenacity and skill of Bartlett and Kataktovik.

The whole account is loaded to the gunnels with adventure, excitement, amusing anecdotes, and details of adaptation and innovation that read like a modern-day *Robinson Crusoe*. For those hooked on the whole "Survival" fad, there can be no better account of a real-life gamble with life and death than *The Last Voyage of the Karluk*.

Frank Holden, who reads *Karluk*, has made himself known throughout Newfoundland as the author and performer of the play *Judge Prowse Presiding*, but he has a long list of credits to his name. Holden's voice is deeper and more educated than Bartlett's was, and thankfully he does not attempt an imitation of Bartlett's famous *Pathé News* style, so he is a real pleasure to listen to. His reading is intelligent, apparently effortless, and low-key without being boring.

When I first began listening to the recording, I

expected more bells and whistles, a bit of music between chapters or sound effects or something. However, the only addition to the text are some footsteps through snow and a reedy fragment of "Red is the Rose" at the beginning and end, and—it was wonderfully gratifying when it arrived—Chopin's "Funeral March," which Bartlett famously played on the Victrola as the *Karluk* went down. In retrospect, I think the choice was wise. The text, particularly the latter chapters, carries the story more than adequately, and it didn't need hotting up.

I have only two caveats with regard to the Rattling Books version of *The Last Voyage of the Karluk*. The first is that, like the book in printed form, it starts off a little slowly. I recall from my first reading that it opened with far too many stodgy details about the purchase of the ship and embarkation at Vancouver. Considering that Bartlett later faced a British Admiralty inquiry which condemned him for having set off to the ice in an inadequate ship, this somewhat pedantic opening is understandable. Bartlett was not just telling a rollicking shipwreck story, he was defending his reputation.

An up-to-date foreword—which one would expect in any modern reprint—could have educated the listener as to the reason for the slow start. The loss of the *Karluk* and the rescue of her crew was a huge news story in 1914, so there was little need for explanation when Bartlett published less than two years later. However, more than a century has since passed, and a five-minute introduction would have been a welcome addition to a fine recording.

Also needed in any edition of *The Last Voyage of the Karluk* is a map of the western Arctic. I have visited Herschel Island and travelled in parts of Alaska, but I still found that I had to dig out a map of the area to figure out exactly where Bartlett was going. The plastic case of the audiobook CD was made to hold a pamphlet or liner notes and could easily have accommodated a map. I wondered if perhaps I had inadvertently received an incomplete copy, but apparently not.

That said, anybody who has even a passing interest in Arctic travel, Inuit culture, Newfoundland history, sailing, survival stories, dog sledding, adventure, or a rollicking good tale will find that after the first twenty minutes, it is impossible to stop listening to *The Last Voyage of the Karluk*. Pop the mp3 into your car player, and it will take you from St. John's to the ferry at Port aux Basques quickly and pleasurably. When you realize that this is approximately the distance Bartlett traveled over the ice to Siberia, you will arrive at your destination with a renewed admiration for the man and his accomplishment.

July 2011

Whenever I think that I've had enough of Mina Hubbard and her tiresome husband, I come across some article or book that revives my interest in this most ladylike explorer. Such was the case with Martha MacDonald's *Very Rough Country*, a collection of articles and essays prompted by the centennial of Mina Hubbard's journey from North West River to Ungava Bay. Half a dozen pages into the book, my Hubbard fatigue had vanished.

For readers unfamiliar with the Hubbard name, Leonidas Hubbard died of hunger and exposure while trying to make his way through the Labrador interior in 1903. His wife, Mina Hubbard, set out in 1905 to complete her husband's failed journey, and she succeeded not only in completing the route, but in racing and beating a far more experienced traveller, her husband's former partner, explorer Dillon Wallace. Since then, but particularly since the early 2000s, Mina has been the subject of biographies, novels, poetry and articles, all documenting and speculating on her journey and what it meant, personally and historically.

A hundred years after her original trip, the Town of North West River, the Labrador Heritage Society, and the Central Labrador Economic Development Board sponsored a number of events to celebrate the anniversary and asked the Labrador Institute at Memorial University to organize an academic symposium in conjunction with these. Martha MacDonald, who worked at the Institute, claimed that she got roped into playing the part of Mina in the reenactment of the journey because she was the only one who could fit into the size six boots that went with the costume.

Whatever the initial impetus, Mina must have really captured MacDonald's imagination, because the Institute put together a dynamic symposium, and MacDonald managed to turn it into an energetic and readable book. I've attended a good-many symposia in my life, and you can believe me when I say that this is not always the outcome.

Part of the success of *Very Rough Country* is due to its broad scope—the symposium was on Labrador exploration, not just on the Hubbard-Wallace feud. The speakers had plenty to say about that, but they also covered the lives and work of A.P. Low, Herman Koehler, and Donald Baxter MacMillan, as well as those of Indigenous people and local trappers. None of the visiting explorers would have come out alive without the knowledge and help of the Innu and Inuit who had travelled the interior without maps for hundreds of years, but you'd be surprised at how invisible they are in most accounts of northern exploration.

Very Rough Country is divided into three parts. The first is, of course, about Mina, and it includes a very successful rendition of a power-point presentation given by the late and greatly missed Anne Hart. The photos are clear, the comments are lively and fresh, and I kept thinking what a fine graphic novel it would make. Five more articles on Mina follow, all of which contain food for thought, but I particularly liked the piece by Roberta Buchanan, who looked at the original diaries and identified what Mina chose to leave out and why.

Part Two looks at other explorers, and the surprise here was the inclusion of a section that was edited out of James West Davidson's and John Rugge's novel *Great Heart*. The excerpt features the diaries of Labrador writer Lydia Campbell, which were published as *Sketches of Labrador Life*, and fans of both books will not want to miss it. The essays on A.P. Low (whose incomplete map Hubbard was using) and Donald MacMillan are full of interesting material, but the prize for this section goes to Peter Armitage for his piece on Herman J. Koehler.

Armitage, though an academic like most of the other contributors to this collection, is anything but stuffy. In fact, at times his article is little short of a rant. Koehler died in Labrador while on a trip through the interior, and for that reason he has often been likened to Leonidas Hubbard, but according to Armitage, the comparison is unfair to Koehler. He traces the tarnish on Koehler's reputation back to journalist Lawrence Millman, whose published work related to the Labrador Innu, Armitage also says, "is stuffed with enough inaccuracy and hyperbole to challenge his credibility in general."

Millman claimed that Koehler was a toilet manufacturer, making him a figure of ridicule, while Armitage asserts that "he made cars, trucks and tractors, and the supposed relevance of toilets is incomprehensible." Once Armitage recovers from his ire, he settles down to a solid, well-documented account of Koehler's career as a very competent explorer whose wife and daughter could probably have given Mina a run for her money when it came to Labrador travel.

The last section of *Very Rough Country* concentrates on the people who were already in Labrador when non-native exploration began. It opens with a transcript of an address by Elizabeth Penashue, mother of a then newly-minted federal cabinet minister, who has been leading walks and canoe trips in the Labrador interior for over two decades. Nobody has ever starved on one of Elizabeth's expeditions, nor has anybody drowned. She was also included on a panel with local explorers Max McLean of North West River and Ron Webb of Nain, who talked about their own travels on the land they and their families had inhabited.

The final two essays overlap slightly. Susan Felsberg gives an overview of the Inuit who were kidnapped or coerced into travelling out of Labrador over the last three or four centuries to become souvenirs, slaves, and exotic exhibits. She argues that people were "Labrador's very first exports" and suggests that as with the minerals, lumber, and hydro that have been harvested for the profit of outsiders, there was very little benefit to Labradorians in these arrangements.

Rainer Baehre's essay, "Ethnological and Anthropological Explorations of the Labrador 'Eskimo' Before 1880," describes some of the same captives as Felsberg and goes on to consider the whole field of racial classification that developed as part of the supposedly scientific study of Indigenous people.

He is particularly interesting on the subject of phrenologists, those people who claimed they could tell a great deal about a society, culture, and race by "reading the skull."

Baehre traces how the scientific community systematically developed criteria designed to prove the superiority of light-skinned Europeans. Moravian missionaries collected skulls from Labrador Inuit which supposedly displayed the "occiput protuberan," associated with the trait of "philoprogenitiveness." In other words, a bump on the head indicative of their love of children was "a sign of the Inuit's inferiority." Their love for their children was attributed to "primal reflexes rather than cognition," so a trait that we normally consider a virtue was considered a fault, "more animal-like than civilized."

In the spirit of full disclosure, I have to admit here that I accompanied Mrs. Penashue to the launch of *Very Rough Country*, though only after I had read the book and written most of this assessment. I noticed that the size six boots Martha MacDonald was wearing at the launch are now held together with duct tape, an indication of how long the journey was from symposium to book. I'd say that like Mina, Martha has emerged from the wilderness victorious, and the Labrador Institute owes her a new pair of boots.

*

July 2011

In 1910, Hesketh Hesketh-Prichard, Geoffrey Gathorne-Hardy, and Robert Porter, two English hunter-explorers and their Newfoundland guide, made their way overland from Nain to Indian House Lake across the Quebec border, and in the process cached a canoe that was no longer of any use to them. Almost a century later, Larry Coady retraced their journey, accompanied by two of their descendants. Coady's memoir of the trip, *The Lost Canoe: A Labrador Adventure,* is of no great historic importance, but it is certainly a great read.

A marine biologist by training, Coady had worked at an arctic char research station in the area earlier in his career. He heard about the Prichard Expedition from a visiting geographer and followed up the reference to Prichard's book, *Through Trackless Labrador,* in the hope of finding information on fish distribution. His attempts to map fish occurrences proved fruitless, because Prichard's route was impossible to decipher.

Thirty years later, Coady was free to pursue his interest in the route Prichard's party had taken. He fixed on the cached canoe as a target for his research, and over the course of several summers, he set out to find whatever might remain of it. I don't usually have much patience with adventure-explorers, historic or current, but Larry Coady never takes himself or his quest too seriously. He recognized that he was on a self-indulgent adventure and wrote about it with appropriate dollops of humour and modesty.

Coady's strength is evident in the opening chapters of *The Lost Canoe*, where he gives a clear and compact summary of the better-known Wallace, Hubbard, and Cabot expeditions that were taking place around the same time as the Prichard trip. From there, he draws readers into both his own trek and Prichard's, battling flies, catching fish, observing bears, and correcting maps.

The photographs in *The Lost Canoe* are of particular interest. Coady juxtaposes photos taken by Prichard with modern ones taken from the same perspective, and aside from the added colour, there are remarkably few differences. Those of us who grew up by the sea are used to dramatic changes in the landscape as a result of erosion, but in the Labrador interior, geologic time moves slowly.

Coady tends to throw around terms like "authentic culture" and "virgin land" with an abandon that would make an anthropologist wince. However, he tells his story with such enthusiasm that you can forgive a certain amount of ethnocentrism. For me, the draw wasn't the elusive canoe or the route, but the epilogue, in which Coady tells us what happened to the original explorers. I won't give anything away except to say that he managed to find some surprising and fascinating biographical information on all three travellers that is worth the price of the book.

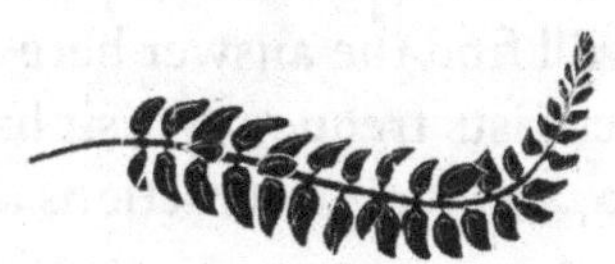

Politics and Activism

Marie Wadden; Nympha Byrne and Camille Fouillard; Gerry Steele; David Natcher, Larry Felt, and Andrea Procter; Gerald Sider

July 2008

WHERE the Pavement Ends: Canada's Aboriginal Recovery Movement and the Urgent Need for Reconciliation, by CBC producer Marie Wadden, is at the opposite end of the spectrum from books like *The Lost Canoe*. It documents Canada's Indigenous recovery movement and the need for reconciliation that is so often talked about but seems to have stalled.

Almost twenty years after publishing Nitassinan, about the Innu struggle to stop low-level flying in Labrador, Wadden has lost none of her dedication and passion. Although *Where the Pavement Ends* has a national perspective, the work is anchored by Wadden's deep knowledge of Labrador. To a great extent, her approach reflects the interconnectedness of Indigenous healers from across the country. Anyone who is wondering why there is a picture of a Plains Cree dancer in a Department of Tourism brochure on Labrador will find the answer here—Indigenous healers and activists frequently visit back and forth across Canada, and their interactions are at the root of the healing movement.

It's often been said that a journalist's job is to explain the problems, not to offer solutions. *Where the Pavement Ends* is a rare case in which a journalist has taken on the chore of voicing the solutions her subjects have come up with. Eleven of the twelve steps towards healing that Wadden describes at the end of this book are natural conclusions given the cross-Canada interviews she has conducted regarding alcoholism, drug addiction, suicide, unemployment, sexual abuse, residential school trauma, and racism.

The twelfth step is Wadden's own expansion on the cultural and healing exchanges that go on within Indigenous communities—Wadden would like to see these exchanges extended to our non-Indigenous youth, to forge friendships and partnerships between the two disparate groups of citizens in this country. Given the high incidence of Fetal Alcohol Syndrome Disorder on the island of Newfoundland, First Nations healers probably have a lot to offer young non-indigenes if only they and their parents can be opened up to such help. The late Apenam Pone said to me, "We participate in your health system, so why shouldn't you participate in ours?"

Much of what Wadden has to say will come as no surprise to people involved even peripherally with Indigenous communities. However, the severity of the fallout from government policies over the years may dismay the bulk of the Canadian public who know little about our First Nations and Inuit citizens. This is not a book that will appeal to readers looking for escapism, but it provides food for thought for those with a conscience who truly want to know what all the fuss is about.

February 2001

I recently came across a well-worn copy of Edith Manuel's *Newfoundland Our Province*, published in 1952. This was the textbook I used in Grade 6. As I flipped through the familiar pages, I thought of how my perception of the province has changed in the intervening years, particularly as it relates to Newfoundland and Labrador's Indigenous people.

Manuel devotes all of two pages to our original inhabitants, supplemented by a drawing of a Beothuk encampment and a section called "Something to Do," which directs students to "use your imagination to make a series of pictures depicting native Indian life in Newfoundland." A lot of imagination was necessary, because thanks to a deliberate government policy, there was almost no information available on Indigenous people in this province. The only natives mentioned as being here before the Europeans are the Beothuk and, the author reluctantly admits, "perhaps in the northern part there were Eskimos." The extent of the ignorance suggested by that "perhaps" really surprised me.

Ignorance is no longer an excuse. Archaeologists have long since confirmed Mi'kmaw claims to seasonal occupation of the west coast, Inuit campsites have been located as far south as Placentia Bay, and the tragedies of Sheshatshiu and Davis Inlet have been played out nightly on our television sets. There was a time when you had to look long and hard to find any published material about our Indigenous citizens. *Them Days* magazine from Happy Valley-Goose Bay went some way towards making people realize that non-Natives share at least part of their history with the Inuit, Innu and Mi'kmaq of the province. Books such as *On the Country: The Micmac of Newfoundland* by Doug Jackson, *Woman of Labrador* by Elizabeth Goudie, and *An Inuk Boy Becomes a Hunter* by John Igloliorte have given more depth to that realization. The year 2000 saw the publication of two more important books: *Remembering the Years of my Life* by Paulus Maggo, and *It's Like the Legend: Innu Women's Voices*.

All of these books deserve attention from the reading public, but *It's Like the Legend* is particularly important, because it comes from a culture about which most Newfoundlanders have known nothing except what appears on television: gas-sniffing children, suicidal teenagers, and alcoholic adults. Having lived in Labrador, I can testify that these television images were true, but they were not all of the truth. Innu life is not so bleak and hopeless. Some of the happiest, most interesting days of my life have been spent among the Innu.

It's Like the Legend, published by Gynergy Books, is a collection of poems, essays, and memoirs by women as diverse as former Mushuau Innu chief Katie Rich, teadoll maker Angela Andrew, police constable Justine Jack, filmmaker Christine Poker, and Elder Cecile Rich. The pieces explore such complex topics as civil disobedience, sobriety, religion, and family relationships in ways most of us can relate to. They take us behind the scenes of those television images.

Elizabeth Penashue writes of being imprisoned for protesting against low-level flying in Goose Bay. We hear about her political convictions, but also about how she was expected to take her meals on the floor of an overcrowded prison cell, next to a filthy open toilet. Mary Adele Andrew, the mother of 15 children, also faced mischief charges. "Over 40 years of forced settlement has been prison enough for me and my family," she declares. Rose Gregoire explains why it was Innu women who led the protests in Goose Bay; marginalized as a woman, excluded from serving on band councils and other "foreign" organizations, "it was almost easier for us, the Innu women, to fight back."

Much of what these women of Sheshatshiu and Davis Inlet write about is political, but they also let us into their personal lives. Rose Gregoire writes movingly about the comfort she derived from the moccasins her mother made for her father. Teenager Natasha Hurley writes about her mixed Innu-settler identity. Cecilia Rich describes coming out as a lesbian. Many of the political essays begin and end with a personal note, reminding us that the hopes and desires of Innu are not very different from those of their non-Innu neighbours.

The book also contains a brief introduction to the Innu, a glossary of common Innu words, a list of place names, and two maps. Each of the short biographies in the back has a photograph and a description of the contributor's life and family. I found myself reading a poem or an essay and then turning back to study the face of the author. When you look at these faces—some old, some young, some pretty, some plain, all individual—it is easy to imagine knowing these women and liking them.

Only one obvious error caught my attention—the editors explain that Katie Rich, Nympha Byrne and Justine Jack were charged and convicted of public mischief. The charge was actually more serious—contempt of court. As one of the accused was a Justice of the Peace, editor Nympha Byrne must have known the difference. Perhaps it just didn't matter to her. Perhaps, as Mary Adele Andrew put it, the "government, the military, the RCMP, as enforcers of these foreign laws, should be facing an Innu judge."

Some of the women who contributed to *It's Like the Legend* have died since the book was published, but their personalities, experiences, and insights live on through the printed pages—another reason older books about Labrador should not be neglected.

February 2012

The title of *Bathtubs but No Water: A Tribute to the Mushuau Innu* by Gerry Steele, comes from a statement made by an Innu Elder in Davis Inlet who claimed that the government had sent toilets and bathtubs to the community, while knowing there was no water there. That just about sums up the attitude to government expressed in this book, and while I tend to agree with the author on most issues, it does seem very one-sided. Perhaps I shouldn't expect balance in a book that has the word "tribute" in the subtitle. Despite his "more in sorrow than in anger" tone, Steele makes no pretense of showing respect for the higher levels of government bureaucracy, although he does have some good words to say about a few of their officials.

Gerry Steele was a consultant hired by Health Canada to advise on the ongoing medical and social problems in Davis Inlet before the community relocated to Natuashish. He gets some of his facts wrong—for example, he claims the women who were charged with contempt of court in 1993 had the charges dropped, when in fact they were found guilty and sentenced to time served—but generally he seems to offer an accurate account of how governments have bungled their dealings with the Innu over and over again.

Steele's basic argument is that the Mushuau Innu

have all the skills needed to run their own finances and healing programs, and the government should simply have handed over the funding and let them get on with it. That may sound a bit irresponsible, but in truth, everything I've seen in Labrador in the last thirty years suggests he is right. Yes, a certain amount of money would have disappeared or been wasted, but it was wasted anyway, without anyone learning anything from it.

What's missing from this account is any sense of what was happening within the Innu community at that time. I have read an account of those events written by an Innu man who was at the centre of the controversial negotiations, and the in-fighting he describes was just as fierce as anything the Innu were leveling at the federal and provincial governments. Steele barely touches on the root of these conflicts when he praises their "kinship-based units" and explains that "only in times of plenty could they afford the luxury of larger groupings, with their more complicated rules of social organization governing both the commercial hunt and the interaction of families and individuals."

James Joyce called Ireland "the sow that eats her farrow," which might not be a bad way of describing the Innu. Like the Irish, however, the Innu forget all their differences when they are up against their colonizers. If you give people their freedom, whether it is from the limits of childhood, prison, or colonization, you run the risk that they are going to make some errors as they adjust to being in charge of their own destinies. If you put so many safeguards in place that they can't make mistakes, it isn't real freedom.

Despite its one-sidedness, *Bathtubs but No Water* lays out the history of the Mushuau Innu's dealing with government fairly clearly. Steele discusses some of the circumstances that led to the various crises, such as the five relocations that small group has endured (from the bush to Old Davis Inlet, to New Davis, to Nutak, back to New Davis, to Natuashish) and the way that Indigenous people were penciled out of the terms of Confederation in 1949.

One of the stated purposes of *Bathtubs but No Water* is "to illustrate how the system failed the Innu." Readers need to focus on that word "how," because I don't think there is any argument that it did fail and the "how," as outlined by Steele, is certainly worth considering. This isn't the last word on the short, sad history of Davis Inlet, but it has some very valid points to make about rural relocation and economic sustainability across Canada.

September 2013

There has been a lot of change in the political and social face of northern Labrador in the last thirty years or so. *Settlement, Subsistence and Change among the Labrador Inuit* is an anthology of essays edited by David Natcher, Larry Felt and Andrea Procter, intended to track that change, particularly as it was brought about by the land claims negotiations that resulted in the establishment of the Nunatsiavut Government. As described by the editors, the book represents "a multidisciplinary exposition of Inuit history, culture and economy" from the perspective of "anthropology, archeology, sociology, biology, environmental studies and geography."

Twenty-six authors contributed to the twelve sections in this book, so I felt safe for once in starting at the middle and working my way randomly through the various parts of the collection. I received the book just as I returned from a visit to Sandwich Bay, where I stayed a gunshot away from the historical site at North River, so I began with the essay by archaeologists Lisa Rankin, Matthew Beaudoin, and Natalie Brewster: "Southern Exposure: The Inuit of Sandwich Bay, Labrador."

Although Inuit travelled and traded with Europeans in Southern Labrador from the 1500s on, there has long been an argument about whether those Inuit who made contact with Basque, French, and English fishers came to the area seasonally to trade or pilfer from the Europeans, or were long-term sojourners or permanent nomadic harvesters in the region. What is certain is that by the eighteenth century, most Southern Inuit had been forced by violence or lured by trade northward to the Moravian mission areas.

Sandwich Bay is considered to be "outside the core Inuit settlement zone," which limits the rights of people in that area with regard to Indigenous land claims. However, if they were traditional users of the area prior to Europeanization, they have every reason to expect their Indigenous rights within the area to be honoured. According to the authors of this essay, recent archaeological findings strongly suggest that Inuit and mixed Inuit-European families had a "significant presence in the Sandwich Bay region since the early seventeenth century and prior to European settlement."

Such findings could have significant ramifications for people who now refer to themselves as NunatuKavummiut with regard to the hunting, fishing and mineral rights of the area. In other words, when Todd Russell complains that the Newfoundland and Labrador government is trampling the Indigenous rights of the people he represents, he's right—they are.

It's interesting that Susan Kaplan identifies the ability to adapt to change by "maintaining a diversity of skills" as well as mental and social flexibility as "the defining characteristics of the Labrador Inuit." I've always thought that diversity of skills, and a refusal to specialize, is what made Newfoundlanders unique in the Canadian mosaic. Peter Whitridge explores how different the Labrador subarctic landscape must have seemed to the Thule Inuit who migrated south from Baffin, every bit as unfamiliar as it was for the Europeans coming from the east mere decades later.

Pete Evans examines the effect of Confederation

on the Inuit of Labrador and quotes Adrian Tanner as saying that "Labrador Inuit probably lost most in the Confederation process because they had more autonomy to lose." Evans's version of the post-Confederation health and welfare of the Inuit certainly supports Tanner's claim. While Inuit who migrated into Labrador of their own free will managed extraordinarily well, Inuit who were resettled south from Nutak and Hebron did not flourish.

Maura Hanrahan's essay on Inuit nutritional literature points out that while Inuit occasionally suffered starvation in the contact era, they did not suffer from malnutrition, unlike settlers to Newfoundland. If they had sufficient food, they had a good diet, but today, although nobody starves, plenty of Inuit have poor health due to dental caries, diabetes, and other nutrition-related diseases.

Given Hanrahan's perspective, it is ironic that an essay by Larry Felt and twelve others on wildlife harvest argues that "subsistence provisioning remains an important strategy of household and community survival" in Labrador. Hunting and distributing wild meat and fish is an important social practice. Members of my own household did not hunt, but were the recipients of a lot of wonderful country food because the children of our Indigenous friends wouldn't eat it.

The essay on climate change in Hopedale, by a team from the University of Guelph, has particular resonance. Apparently local residents identified changes in sea ice formation as their most significant concern. Subsequent to the study, one of the most experienced and knowledgeable hunters in Hopedale drowned when his skidoo broke through harbour ice that he had judged to be solid. Other pieces in the book cover land use planning, the impact of uranium mining on communities, the politics of wildlife harvesting, the position of Elders in Indigenous government, and ethnic membership in Nunatsiavut.

Some of the material in these essays, such as that on methodology, is pretty dry reading for the layman, and the styles are often academic and dense. For example, Peter Whitridge uses the word "imaginaries" as a noun but does not define it. However, you can generally puzzle out the gist of the arguments. *Settlement, Subsistence and Change* contains a great deal of important information. It is to be hoped that writers who straddle the divide between academic and popular publications will make this information more accessible to the general reading public in years to come.

July 2014

I approached Gerald Sider's book *Skin for Skin: Death and Life for Inuit and Innu*, with some reluctance. When I saw the title, I just thought, "If I never have to go to another funeral for a child who has committed suicide, it will be too soon." I don't know how a parent can survive such intolerable pain, and I don't understand why our government doesn't declare the epidemic of suicide we are suffering in Labrador to be a disaster and take emergency measures. Gerald Sider takes this emergency seriously, and although he doesn't know how to stop it, Sider at least believes he understands why it is happening, which is more than most people in government can say.

Although it is published by an academic press, *Skin for Skin* is a volume that everyone who interacts with the Indigenous communities in this province should read, including the Innu and Inuit themselves, if possible. The voice is passionate, intense, and very personal, bordering on aggressively confrontational at times. However, anyone who can remain objective when children are dying has nothing to say that will be of any use, and there are times when anger is the only reasonable response. Sider traces the roots of the epidemic of suicide among native youth back to colonial times when the fur trade was active, and argues that the Hudson's Bay Company and Moravian policies of underpaying and undersupplying Innu and Inuit led to famines, dependency, and ultimately self-destruction.

The book is not based on field work or "participant observation," but is grounded in intense library and archive research and conversations with others who have done field work, such as Carol Brice-Bennett and Peter Armitage. I was particularly struck by how much information Sider extracted from the papers of Father Edward O'Brien, known in Labrador as Father Whitehead. There is a tendency today to dismiss anything written by missionaries and a lot of important data is ignored as a result.

Sider begins his consideration of the suicide epidemic with a summary of the history of colonization in Labrador, first by France and England and later by Newfoundland itself. I have read a fair bit of Labrador anthropology and history, but I had not really understood that the Innu, like the Beothuks, were driven away from the coast by fishermen, whalers, and traders, as well as violent confrontations with Inuit, so that they retreated to the interior where inadequate food supplies and endemic disease decimated them almost into extinction. It was also helpful to be reminded that the Labrador Inuit, who had long resided on the coast below the treeline where they hunted small whales, lived very different lives from the Inuit of Boothia or Baffin.

One of Sider's basic arguments is that Indigenous anger arises from caring intensely for their children. To live in what youth call "concentration villages," with dirt roads, inadequate housing, poor nutrition, and a failing education system, and to feel you can do nothing about it, creates anger. To have to face the needs of your family day after day, without the means to meet those needs, creates anger. This anger then overflows onto those whose very existence is an affront to the caregivers.

It's Sider's contention that Indigenous people in Labrador have suffered so much in the last two centuries, but particularly since the 1930s, that they are experiencing a form of post-traumatic stress disorder. I remember that when I first came to Labrador about thirty years ago, young people in Nain used to refer to their home as "Viet Nain." Clearly, they felt they were living in a war zone, with the body count rising daily. Those Viet Nainers are now the parents of the children who are dying today.

Sider accepts the generally-held belief that it was Innu protest that helped stop low-level flying in Labrador, but actually it was the fall of the Iron Curtain in 1989-90, followed by the introduction of drones, that brought an end to the flights. Nevertheless, Sider raises the possibility that "people do not have to actually take control of their lives to give themselves a healing, or partially healing, dignity." Protests do not have to succeed to be successful, because the protests themselves make people feel powerful.

Sider also suggests that empowering Indigenous people might be good for the colonizers as well, in the long run. If Indigenous rights had been recognized when Newfoundland was negotiating the deal with Hydro Quebec, then the entire benefits of the development could not have gone to Quebec. Instead, "in diminishing Native people, they [the Newfoundland government] diminished themselves even more."

There are, inevitably in such a wide-ranging and complex work, errors. Sider seems to have mixed up Dr. Helge (not Helga) Kleivan with his widow, Dr. Inge Kleivan; St. Anthony's medical facility was not "a small cottage hospital" in 1977; and prior to 1949, Newfoundland did not refuse to recognize Indigenous people in Labrador "since they could vote," as nobody in Newfoundland or Labrador could vote for a legislature under Commission of Government. Sedna is not just an Alaskan mythic figure; she is known throughout the circumpolar world under a variety of names and guises with versions of the story varying even within small communities. The Innu who were flooded out by the Smallwood Reservoir didn't live in small cabins, but were semi-nomadic hunters who did a little trapping on the side. These are relatively minor errors in a much larger and generally accurate picture.

I cannot pretend that I understood and retained all of Sider's arguments in *Skin for Skin.* He has a lot to say about a great many things, some of them over my head, but I did welcome a fresh, angry voice from someone who, like me, thinks it is intolerable that so many children are taking their own lives in Labrador.

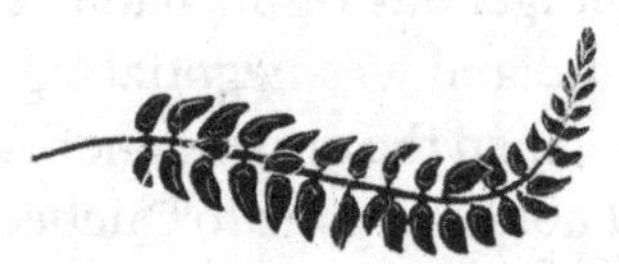

The Land

David Liverman; Arnold Zageris; Steve Bruneau; the Labrador Institute and Derek Wilton; Wilfred Grenfell; Edward Caldwell Moore

May 2007

I have, over the years, had ample exposure to scientific writing about the north and its geography, but that writing is often incomprehensible to me, even when the phenomenon being discussed is right under my nose, and I am always glad when I encounter a writer who can convey the tremendous power of a landscape without giving me a headache. Non-scientists with an eye for nature, such as the late Leonard Budgell, are few and far between, but if a scientist can motivate a reader to learn about the environment, in words the layman can understand, it is a gift.

I began reading David Liverman's *Killer Snow: Avalanches in Newfoundland and Labrador*, in a canvas tent, in four feet of rain-soaked snow, at the foot of a steep ridge near Sheshatshiu. By the time the sun set, I was calculating the angle of the slope and reviewing what kind of weather had preceded my impromptu overnight visit to the Penashue family's camp. That's the kind of book this is—it makes you think about fairly ordinary situations in ways you had never considered before.

Because I have a vivid recollection of the tragic Battery avalanche of 1959 in which five people died, including a boy about my own age, I didn't need much convincing to believe that avalanches are more common in the province than most people think. In fact, Liverman believed that at the time he was writing, "the historical risk of dying in an avalanche in Newfoundland and Labrador [was] considerably higher than the Canadian average, and likely as high as or higher than British Columbia."

Death by avalanche is not the first thing that enters your head when your youngster goes out sliding on a fine winter morning, nor the last thing that comes to mind when you hunker down by the wood stove on a snowy winter night. Liverman suggests that sometimes it should be. Considering the increased popularity of winter tourism and sports, and the fact that we have the highest per capita ownership of snowmobiles in the country (probably the world), we should be taking avalanches seriously.

Those with a taste for stories of death, doom, and miraculous escape will find plenty to enjoy in this book, which outlines the facts about more than fifty avalanches. Liverman's clear and simple explanations of the physics behind the phenomenon will not deter even the most unscientific among us, and his diagrams of how to approach a potential avalanche area should be posted on the walls of every cabin and tilt in the province.

What strikes me most about this simple and captivating book is Liverman's approach to the whole subject. He readily admits that his curiosity about avalanches was initially piqued by a tombstone he saw in Tilt Cove which memorializes the deaths of mine superintendent Francis James Williams and his thirteen-year-old son James Sharrock, who were killed by a snowslide in 1912. Obviously Liverman has the heart of a poet.

When government records failed to answer the questions posed by these deaths, Liverman and his colleagues turned to the archives and to oral history, and there he found most of the information that makes up the substance of *Killer Snow*. Engineers at C-CORE, Memorial's cold ocean resources institute, did the same thing when trying to learn about iceberg behavior, and it is an approach that perhaps more of our fisheries scientists should emulate as well.

Traditional ecological knowledge, now known by the acronym TEK, is a popular panacea these days. Throw in a few obscure words of wisdom from some old geezer on a stagehead or a First Nations Elder at a sweatlodge, and the public thirst for something they can relate to is assuaged. In this case, however, the sudden onset, the surprising power, and the devastating impact of avalanches are better conveyed by the first-person accounts of avalanche survivors and the relatives of those who didn't make it out of the snow than by all the charts and statistics Liverman can muster.

Anyone who goes out snowmobiling, snowboarding, or skiing in this province should read this book, as should parents whose children are active in winter sports. It can change behaviour, however marginally, and might save a life. In my own case, sober second thought convinced me that the lack of a gully and the presence of trees on the slope behind the tent I was sleeping in were indicators that I was unlikely to be buried in the night. However, just in case, I moved my sleeping bag well to one side of the tin stove. In Newfoundland, at least, victims of snowslides are almost as likely to be burned to death as smothered or frozen. Not a comforting thought.

June 2014

The opening photograph in Arnold Zageris's new book *On the Labrador* is typical of the images in this gorgeous publication. Covering two large pages, it features huge dark boulders on the right, smooth, pale beach stones on the left, and in the background, across a tickle, a long, grey stretch of mountains. Take a closer look and you will notice a sprinkling of lichen—red, white and orange—plus a tiny flowering plant hidden in a crack of rock.

There are photos like this all the way through *On the Labrador*, huge sweeping views with a dusting of snow in the foreground, or a trail of beach pea or a caribou track. At other times, the photos are so close and intense that if you did not have the titles, you might be unable to distinguish rock from sky or sky from water. Zageris is the first photographer I've encountered who has been able to capture the northern landscape as I've seen it over the last five decades. I love Richard Harrington or Ulli Steltzer's shots of people, and Mike Beedell's animals, but Zageris captures the Arctic or subarctic tundra as no one else has.

Zageris used a large format, 4×5 camera, which requires individually prepared film holders and working under a rubber dark cloth, like the photographers in old cowboy movies. I know nothing about the technology, but the results are phenomenal. His best shots appear to be startlingly simple; shattered rock, weathered granite, a growler in a vast black sea, or a scarlet blush of seal's blood in the water. There are a few people in these photos, showing off the thick swarms of nippers or handling a boat, but generally the figures are only there to give a sense of proportion. You often have to search a landscape before locating a tiny figure that suddenly makes you realize the magnitude of the scene.

Although photographs comprise the majority of this book, Zageris devotes a fair proportion to text, describing how he became interested in Labrador, where he went on his sixteen visits north, and how he set up his shots. Some of this is intriguing, such as the stories of how he used his socks to improvise an anchor for his tripod on one trip, and to stop a hole in his boat on another. Some stories are less successful.

I would guess that either Zageris or the publishers felt that at least some shots of the settlements and the people who live in them were necessary for balance, but he hasn't got anything special to offer in these areas. His photos of Nain are unremarkable, and what little interaction he apparently had with local Inuit is very superficial. His accounts of these moments seem strained and unsure.

His prose is much better when he is describing setting up his photographs, what the weather did to the light, and how he got himself out of a number of quite serious scrapes. He almost lost his boat to a high tide on one occasion, came near foundering under an iceberg, and at least once got disoriented and lost his way. These passages give some idea of the personality needed to wait hours, days, or even years for a perfect shot of a given site.

Sometimes, I had to read and reread sentences to try and understand their meaning. What are "boulders of less than stable rock" or what does "a pile of flat rock slabs . . . each precariously close to its angle of repose" mean? I can guess—unstable boulders, precarious slabs—but I would prefer to have been sure. In at least four other cases, I decided the obscurity was caused by a typographical error. There are other errors as well. He calls St. Anthony "Port" Anthony and misidentifies Montagnais for Naskapis, when really neither name is appropriate any longer. Even the media release that came from the publishers with my review copy of the book got off to a bad start with the claim that Sebastian Cabot dubbed Labrador the land God gave to Cain. It was actually Jacques Cartier, 37 years after John Cabot sighted land in North America. I don't know that Cabot made it anywhere near to Labrador.

Generally when I encounter typos or errors in a text, I mark a correction in the margin, but in this case, the book is beautiful and the problems relatively minor, so my copy of *On the Labrador* is still pristine. I mention this so as not to discourage anyone from buying it, but at $60 a copy, I think the publishers could have been a bit more rigorous in their proofreading.

Zageris has a science background, and I often wished he had tapped into it more than into his poetic side, particularly with regard to the titles and captions on his landscape photographs. For example, a small, striking shot of an evening sky carries the caption, "Some fiery sunsets in Labrador can actually look nuclear. Which, in fact, they are." This didn't make sense to me, and not just because of the nonstandard punctuation. Perhaps there is some scientific phenomenon I am unaware of that he might have explained.

The bottom line, however, is that you can just ignore the text after a quick once-over, and concentrate on the images. The big slabs of cliff-face, the stark, bleached remains of an ancient spruce, and the mineral-stained or lichen-encrusted tumbles of boulders can't be ignored, and I will be going back to this book again and again, especially now that my own Arctic sojourning days are nearing an end.

When a local luminary in Goose Bay retired, his staff gave him a copy of this book as a farewell gift. The book had only just made its way into the shops there, and most Labradorians had yet to see it, but judging by the reception that copy got, it will be a favourite presentation gift for a long time to come. However, don't wait for someone to give it to you—give yourself a present and crack some of the mystery of what draws people from distant places to spend time in Labrador.

October 2010

I can't say enough good things about Steve Bruneau's field guide entitled *Icebergs of Newfoundland and Labrador*. This is a fifth, "new colour" edition, and I confess to never having seen the first four editions, but I would guess that the colour is a terrific improvement. I have written in praise of Bruneau's layman's guides to icebergs before but cannot miss the opportunity to heap a little more praise on his ever-humble head.

He begins with a short Q&A section, answering the most frequently asked queries he gets about icebergs, and follows it with a fascinating assemblage of really neat facts and trivia that I can't even begin to sum up, as the entries are too unbelievable and it might spoil the fun for readers. The third part is a mini-anthology of historic iceberg literature, which I admit slowed me down a bit, but it is redeemed by the section called "Humorous E-mails Received by the Author." Part 4 is a quick checklist of how to get ready to go hunting icebergs.

Part 5 of *Icebergs of Newfoundland and Labrador* contains the meat and potatoes of the book—the illustrations. And what illustrations they are. There are lots of colour photos as well as sketches and charts outlining everything from iceberg characteristics to lighting effects, shape, deterioration, safety, travel and more. This is the first time I've come across an explanation of why icebergs look black at certain times, and there is a brief lesson on how to sketch an iceberg that had me reaching for a pencil.

I was going to write that *Icebergs of Newfoundland and Labrador* is an absolute necessity for every B&B and tourist operation in the province, but on reflection I will amend that to every household in the province. Why save the good stuff for the tourists? This is the best book of its kind I've seen anywhere in years. It's going on my "No, you can't borrow it" shelf.

April 2010

The Polar Bear in the Rock by the Labrador Institute and Derek Wilton is a hard book to categorize. It's a little bit of a number of things—a non-fiction academic account of the geology of Labrador, the traditional Inuit account of how a striking landmark was formed, a picture book for children, and an Inuttitut and Innu-aimun text for language teachers and Elders.

Briefly, the book tells how a white boulder resembling a polar bear came to be formed in the vicinity of Nain. Derek Wilton explains how magma flowed upward through the earth's crust to produce anorthite crystals which were scraped clean by glaciers and moved and bleached by weathering. His explanations are simple, factual, and short enough not to be daunting.

The Inuit storytellers' account is that a polar bear came and threatened the Inuit women and children who were fishing at Annainak Brook while their men were away. A crippled old man beat a drum, which turned the bear into a rock. This traditional creation myth is accompanied by very pleasant illustrations by Cynthia Colosimo, an artist from Forteau. The text makes no value judgement about which account is accurate, nor is there any examination of what the Inuit story means or what values it embodies.

Stories of people and animals being turned to stone abound in all cultures. Bruno Bettleheim argues that being turned to stone stands for "a lack of true humanity, an inability to respond to higher values." This interpretation is certainly valid for the Inuit stories of stone people I have heard in other parts of the north. Children turn to stone for lying or stealing, but most stone adults result from their refusal to marry, a denial of human emotion and mutual need. Among the Ammassalik Inuit of Greenland, the Orssuiaq or blubberstone, usually a stone woman, is a shiny, white feldspar, like the Nain bear stone.

I've no idea what the Nain story means, although clearly it has something to do with procreation and fecundity. It is interesting that it is while the men are away that the bear comes threatening the women. The magic of the drum, the importance of the elderly and the disabled, and the mutual cooperation of the two genders are all values that are evident in the story, but my guess is that it is a far more complex tale than is suggested in this book for children.

My only quarrel with this work is that, like a lot of books written by committees, it is a bit bland, a bit too clean and ironed flat. Most Inuit tales have some puzzling elements, odd bits that function almost like riddles. I find these mysterious elements drive me to dig deeper into the tale, pushing me into a culture that is unfamiliar and interesting. Unfortunately, most educators worry that such untidy turns in the narrative will frustrate children, so they remove all obstacles. At least Derek Wilton gave them something substantial to chew on. Still, if you want to get a closer look at the science and culture of Northern Labrador, there is plenty to challenge a reader of any age in *The Polar Bear in the Rock*. The Inuttitut and Innu-aimun texts alone could keep me busy for years.

*

October 2004

I cannot remember when I first read Wilfred Grenfell's *Adrift on an Icepan*, but I was probably no more than ten years old, and perhaps in my twenties when I read it again. Second time around, I was almost certainly a little more skeptical of the hearty tone of adventure that permeates the account, but I still found it a gripping tale. For those few who haven't encountered this classic story of survival, it recounts the experience of the famous northern doctor on an occasion when he was called to a sick boy and got carried out to sea on the ice. It was Easter Sunday morning, 1908, a warm April day, and with typical bravado, Grenfell travelled by dogteam ahead of his guides, became separated from them, and drifted away.

Two days later he was rescued at the mouth of Hare Bay, having sacrificed several of his dogs to fashion makeshift clothing and a flag. He was cold and hungry, his feet were frostbitten, and he had suffered several dog bites, but he was otherwise unharmed. The following day, he dictated an account of his near-fatal adventure which was published in the *New York Tribune*.

I have no idea how many copies of what came to be known as *Adrift on an Icepan* were eventually published, but demand for the book seemed to be inexhaustible and it probably carried the Grenfell Mission budget for a good many years. According to Ron Rompkey, it went through eighteen editions in the first ten years, and when new plates were struck for it in 1920, that particular edition alone sold 58,000 copies.

Almost a hundred years later, Rattling Books brought out a 62-minute CD recording of the small book, narrated and produced by Chris Brookes. The text is interspersed with hymns of the period by Isaac Watts, Sir Arthur Sullivan and others, played by Christina Smith on violin. Jay Roberts provides the voice of George Andrews, one of the rescuers, and Janis Spence provided an introduction and acting direction.

I'm not sure exactly what it is about this story that makes it so compelling, but it retains its hold on the imagination to this day. There is the obvious drama of the do-good doctor imperiled in the course of his duty; there is the appeal of the dogs, brave dumb beasts who trust their master even as he cuts their throats; there is the *Robinson Crusoe* detail of making-do with what is at hand in an emergency. But it goes beyond that. The story-telling technique is akin to *The Perils of Pauline* film serials. Grenfell manages to rig up a harness but "alas," it isn't long enough. He finds a slightly larger pan on which to take refuge, but "unfortunately" he can't get the dogs to go to it. Each time, he uses his ingenuity to hang on another hour, but alas and unfortunately, each time is thwarted by merciless nature. But he never gives up.

It is probably no coincidence that 1908 was the year Ralph Connor's first volume of fiction was published. Connor, a proponent of Muscular Christianity, wrote stories in which physical courage was matched by moral courage, and Christian principles always won in the end. It may sound stuffy, but it wasn't—to this day I can recall the wild ride through the woods of *The Man from Glengarry*, as vividly as I remember the Headless Horseman in pursuit of Ichabod Crane in *The Legend of Sleepy Hollow*. All of which is intended to convince you that *Adrift on an Icepan* is no dull Christian tract, but a ripping good adventure that will hold the attention of people of all ages and genders.

Viewers of Varrick Frissell's film *The Viking*, which was released on video some years back, will recall that Wilfred Grenfell had a high, somewhat weak voice. Janis Spence has taken this straw and spun it into gold. Chris Brookes' thready pipes and somewhat English intonations are perfect for Grenfell, but by adopting an intimate, slightly tongue-in-cheek modulation, he catches the magic that made the doctor one of the most sought-after lecturers in North America. You feel like you are holed up in a tilt or an igloo on a nasty night, with this fascinating man murmuring his story into your ear.

It intrigued me to read in Ron Rompkey's biography of Grenfell that while the doctor claimed after the fact that he shook the incident off like water off a duck's back, in reality he was a mess, moving like someone twice his age, huddling by the stove, and requiring sedation and morphine to put him to sleep. "The mental trauma of facing his own extinction had made him uncharacteristically moody," wrote Rompkey. "Thus he overreacted to trivial events and became periodically depressed."

A century ago, the addendum by George Andrews, "rendered into an approximation of northern Newfoundland dialect" as Rompkey put it, might have seemed just a quaint confirmation of Grenfell's courage. Today, it reads a bit differently. You don't need to be a mental genius to realize that accidentally falling into a dangerous situation, as happened to Grenfell, is somewhat different from deliberately putting yourself into potential harm as his rescuers did. Obviously, the real hero wasn't the doctor who worked to save his own life, but the men like Andrews who imperiled their own lives to save another. And while Jay Roberts doesn't work to put an ironic spin on his reading, the fact that Grenfell rewarded his rescuers with framed photographs of himself speaks volumes.

The acting, the music, the beautiful cover design by John Andrews, and the excellent quality of the sound all combine in a classic recording of a classic tale, proof if it were needed that Newfoundland can produce world-class works of literary and technological merit. I can confidently recommend this CD as a nostalgia or historic icon, but that would be selling it short. Grenfell might have had his weaknesses and faults, but Rattling Books's *Adrift on an Icepan* is a timely reminder that he was a dynamite storyteller who could twist and manipulate his listeners with the best of them. A century later, he can still work the magic, and you might even find yourself reaching for your cheque book. If so, use it to buy another

Rattling Books CD; or if you still prefer your books made from paper, *Adrift on an Ice Pan* was also republished in print in 2016 by Flanker Press.

May 2009

An interesting take on Grenfell's adventures in Labrador comes from one of the many volunteers he invited to accompany him on the ship he used to make his medical rounds in the summers. In 1905 the Rev. Edward Caldwell Moore volunteered to travel along the Labrador coast with Grenfell "to participate in and lead worship, and to help Grenfell in any ways that presented during the cruise." For seven weeks Moore gave sermons, observed medical operations, sorted stores, loaded wood, and generally made himself useful. He also pined for his wife and children, obsessed over mail delivery and telegraph facilities, learned a lot about life on the coast, and wrote letters and a journal about his experiences.

Those letters and journal are now available to the general reader as *A Trip to Labrador*, thanks to the dedication and efforts of Kirby Walsh, a native of Cartwright now living in Nova Scotia, who transcribed and edited them into a publishable manuscript. By cutting out irrelevant passages, such as 24 pages of directions from Moore to his wife about paying bills while he was gone, Walsh has provided us with a fairly lively and interesting snapshot of life in Labrador and aboard the mission ship *Strathcona* at that time.

Unknown to Moore until the trip was over, Grenfell had received a better offer that summer—a chance to impress and influence Governor Sir William McGregor, who was travelling the coast on board the *Fiona*. Grenfell was willing to sacrifice the goodwill of his numerous volunteers during that cruise in order to ingratiate himself with the Newfoundland authorities, and his constant changes of plans to accommodate the officials puzzled and distressed Moore. Grenfell's attempts to curry favour with the governor backfired badly after Grenfell ran the *Fiona* (which Moore spells *Faiona*) onto a shoal, but despite everything, Moore continued to be loyal to the doctor and his aims. However, perhaps because that loyalty was one-sided, Moore gives us a warts-and-all portrait of a man who has been alternately demonized and deified in Newfoundland and Labrador.

Life aboard the *Strathcona* was not easy, particularly for somebody as meticulous and as obsessive as Moore. She was eighty feet long and equipped with medical cots, dispensary, and x-ray equipment, but she had no hold for freight, was overcrowded, and her crew were amateurs. Grenfell insisted upon running her engines on wood, so the deck was usually piled high with firewood as well as freight and lumber. Grenfell is described as erratic, disorderly, intolerant, poorly organized, incapable of delegating work, and "indifferent to dirt." "Nothing is so bad about the boat as the dirt," writes Moore. "She is filthy—I cannot say less—She can hardly be less so long as she is a menagerie—and G. is so devoted to his pets." Grenfell had on board no fewer than five dogs and, by the end of the cruise, fifteen foxes, all of which defecated on the deck and drove the men crazy. Meals were haphazard, and likely to be delayed to accommodate Grenfell, who wanted a bath or who felt the need to pray for the conversion of the Jews, while everyone else on board starved.

Over and over again, Moore comments on Grenfell's inability to think ahead, to stick to a decision, or to delegate authority. Grenfell was apparently indifferent to the hard work and planning of his volunteers, whimsical in his enthusiasms, overconfident of his own abilities and, in Moore's words, "a man of highest motive but not wise nor always just." Moore goes on to describe him as "Impulsive and unreliable often making representations and holding out expectations etc. wh[ich] he cannot possibly keep."

Despite his disappointment in Grenfell, Moore clearly admires the man, who had a charisma that simply bound people to him and held them in thrall. But if Grenfell was such a terrible leader, how did he hold things together for so long? My own guess is that he had the good fortune or the good sense to marry a woman who was able to undo many of his mistakes and paper over many of his flaws. If even half of what Moore wrote about Grenfell was true, the whole organization was heading for disaster, and only the money and organizational influence of

Anne MacClanahan, whom he married three years later, prevented that disaster.

A Trip to Labrador is a fascinating read for anyone with the slightest interest in Labrador or the Grenfell Mission. The introduction and footnotes supplied by editor Kirby Walsh are helpful, and the insight he offers from his own experiences add to the text. The cover is attractive, the bibliography is useful, and there is an index. This is a fine little book.

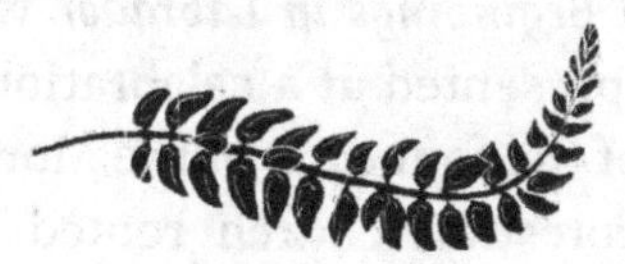

The Moravian Experience

Hans Rollmann; Abraham Ulrikab;
France Rivet; Carol Brice-Bennett

June 2010

MORAVIAN *Beginnings in Labrador* was compiled from papers presented at a celebration of the 550th anniversary of the founding of the Moravian Brotherhood, a Protestant church rooted in Northern Bohemia. The Moravians had a policy of worldwide missionary outreach and began their work among Inuit in Labrador in 1752. Today there are hundreds of Moravian adherents living in Labrador, distributed among the four congregations of Nain, Hopedale, Makkovik, and Happy Valley-Goose Bay.

Most of the essays collected in this volume seem to be pointing out that the political and religious history of Labrador goes back farther and is more complex than is generally assumed. Contributors consider the Labrador boundary, the land grants given to the missionaries, the complications caused by mixing trade and Christianization, Moravian religious beliefs and practices, and how and why the missionaries kept the extensive archives for which they are famous.

Land grants and boundaries are not usually my

favourite subjects for recreational reading, but a basic understanding of both is necessary for a fuller understanding of Labrador history, and both Hans Rollmann and Jim Hiller make acquiring this knowledge a fairly painless experience. With these subjects under my belt, I was better able to enjoy the other essays in the book.

John C. Kennedy argues that the southern Labrador Inuit were essentially Dorset hunters and traders while the Northern Labrador Inuit were Thule whalers. Much of the material in this essay was covered by Garth Taylor's more popular writings some years ago, but I don't think I fully understood the significance of that distinction for Labrador before. Kennedy's essay goes some way towards explaining why the mixed-heritage descendants of these Dorset people generally denied a relationship with their northern neighbours in previous centuries. It's not that they weren't Inuit, it was that they weren't that kind of Inuit.

Taylor himself contributes a most interesting account of Jens Haven's 1764 reconnaissance journey to Labrador. Haven went via St. John's, where he met with Governor Palliser and obtained a proclamation, ordering settlers not to harass or murder Inuit. Again, this proclamation was something I had read about before, but because I had not realized the extent of the hostilities between the two groups, I had not seen how important it was. Without Haven's and Palliser's intercession, the Inuit might have had the same fate as the Beothuks. The account of

Haven's journey reads like a cross between a French farce and *Pilgrim's Progress*, full of drama and humour.

Archaeology buffs, and those readers who just take an interest in old houses, will be intrigued by Henry Cary's account of the first mission house near Makkovik. After the death of Johann Christian Erhardt and the six sailors of the *Hope*, the site was abandoned and eventually plundered, and later still the location was lost. However, Labradorians are great ones for oral history, and when a student heard Hans Rollmann discuss the unknown location, she suggested that he consult her father, Mr. Ted Andersen of Makkovik. Andersen was able to take Rollmann directly to the spot, just as George Decker had led Helge Ingstad to the Viking ruins at L'Anse-aux-Meadows, and the site was eventually excavated. There are lots of high-quality illustrations included with this piece, and I pored over them gladly. *Moravian Beginnings* is an academic volume, and I was forced to consult a dictionary on several occasions, but on the whole the work is accessible to any keen reader, and I highly recommend it.

June 2006

In 1880, a European entrepreneur named Johan Adrian Jacobsen came to Labrador and recruited eight Inuit to go with him to Hamburg and perform as living anthropological exhibits in a human zoo. The Inuit were strongly advised by the Moravian missionaries not to attempt this venture, but they went anyway, lured by curiosity and promises of payment. Unfortunately, Jacobsen forgot to have his exotic employees vaccinated against smallpox, which was rampant in parts of Germany at the time, and they all caught the disease and died. One of them, Abraham Ulrikab, wrote letters and a small diary, which made its way back to Labrador where it was translated from Inuttitut into German.

A hundred years later, Garth Taylor found the translation, and he published an article on the diary in *Canadian Geographic* magazine, including excerpts in English produced with the help of his wife. That's where I first encountered Abraham and his fellow travelers, and I was so taken by the story that I tried to get various academics interested in the work, with no success until I passed it on to Hartmut Lutz, a German scholar who was visiting Canada at the time.

Over the next twenty years, Lutz and a group of his students retranslated the German version of Abraham's diary and collected newspaper accounts and contemporary and modern commentaries and photographs to present as full a picture of what happened to this small group of Inuit, and why, as it is possible to have 140 years after the fact.

Lutz uses the case of Abraham and his family to trace the ways that pseudo-science such as phrenology later moved from "lofty idealism to concrete discrimination," sowing the seeds of racism that culminated in the Holocaust half a century later. The subsequent deaths of the eight Inuit provided a tragic postscript to the events, but even if they had returned home safely, the ethical debate over "displaying our equals in zoos" would still have been relevant.

Inuit artist and author Alootook Ipellie makes it clear in his foreword to the book that not much has really changed in the last 100 years or more. He writes that when Iyola Kingwatsiak was invited to participate in a conference on Inuit art at the McMichael Gallery in Kleinburg, Ontario, he found he was expected to sit and say nothing, like "art in a showcase display." If you doubt Ipellie's contention that Indigenous people are "still treated as exotic specimens," you must have missed the meet-and-greet opportunities when Innu set up tents on the grounds of the Arts and Culture Centre and The Rooms in St. John's not so many years ago.

What is extraordinary is not that we still expect Indigenous people to display themselves, but that they are still willing to do it. And thank God for that, because if Elizabeth Penashue ever decided to take up arms and lead a violent revolution instead of dishing up tea, bannock, and gentle persuasion, I wouldn't give our government very good odds to win.

While *The Diary of Abraham Ulrikhab* is essentially an account of a tragedy, there are some light moments. Included are several advertisements for the "Golden 110," Berlin's version of the Big Six store. Ulrike is depicted in these ads as exhorting her husband Abraham to discard his out-of-fashion sealskin parka and dress up like a dandy in a Kaiser coat. He obligingly runs right down to the Leipziger Straße and fills his bags with half-price suits and dressing gowns, "given away as good as free."

Abraham Ulrikab's is the earliest known Labrador Inuit diary ever written. It is a fascinating read, made more interesting by the addition of the historic and current photographs, including some beautiful work by Hans-Ludwig Blohm. This is a book that should be in every school and library in the province, for it is said that if we do not know our history, we are doomed to repeat it. This is one episode we don't want to see happen again.

December 2014

France Rivet's book, *In the Footsteps of Abraham Ulrikab,* builds upon the previous works by Taylor and Lutz, and it is not really complete without them. True, she does include extracts from both commentaries in her own book, but there is little of the context and analysis that Lutz provides. Instead we are given raw research and left to make of it what we may.

The heart of the story is a simple one of hubris.

Abraham, a devoted husband and father, wishes to better his situation, so he takes his family on what is to be an exciting adventure, only to find that the pressure of being exhibited to thousands of people each day is more stressful and exhausting than he could have imagined. Then, one by one, he watches his children, his wife, his nephew, and his friends die, until he dies himself.

To this story, France Rivet adds the pseudo-scientific background that justified exhibiting human beings like animals in a zoo. Adrian Jacobsen, who also robbed graves and sold body parts, justified his participation as promoting education. Carl Hagenbeck, who developed and sponsored the ethnographic exhibits, claimed that his shows promoted cultural understanding. The doctors who measured skulls, made brain casts, and autopsied bodies were merely broadening medical knowledge for the benefit of humanity.

A clear bias is evident in the documents of that time, which Rivet reproduces here in English. The Inuit are compared with various animals such as horses and chimpanzees. They are consistently described as ugly, despite the evidence of the photographs, which show eight exceptionally good-looking people. They are repeatedly described as inferior, degraded, defective, or of limited intelligence. You have to go back to Hartmut Lutz to understand that here were the seeds of racial classification that culminated half a century later in the Nazi Third Reich.

Rivet claims that her aim in writing the book was

to uncover the events of 1880-81, and she does do that, tracking the movements of the exhibition, the origins of museum collections, reproducing newspaper accounts, and describing her own various discoveries. However, she doesn't interpret what she finds for the reader's benefit. Even with the help of my father-in-law's old medical dictionary, I was unable to understand the implications of the report on the three brain casts taken after the Inuit died. When the scientists refer to the "poor differentiation of the convolutions and the simple character of the sulci, especially over the frontal lobes," I have no idea what that means. Some interpretation of the autopsy findings would have been useful, even if it was simply to debunk outdated medical beliefs.

Rivet's major discovery—and it is a significant one—was when she located the skeletons of five of the Inuit, stripped down and articulated for exhibition in the National Museum of Natural History in Paris. The bodies had been exhumed five years after their burial and included in a new Gallery of Anthropology.

At this point, it is necessary to consult more recent publications than Rivet's book, because the story isn't over. According to an article in *Labrador Life* magazine, Rivet immediately alerted the Nunatsiavut Government, the Canadian Government, and the French and German diplomatic authorities in Canada to the existence of the skeletons, so that negotiations could begin for repatriation of the remains.

In 2011, the remains of 22 Inuit which had been illegally exhumed from the Christian cemetery at Zoar were repatriated from a museum in Chicago. At the reinternment, Johannes Lampe called the actions of anthropologist William Duncan Strong, who had stolen the bodies, "immoral, disrespectful and disgraceful." The same could certainly be said for the treatment of Abraham Ulrikab's people, and repatriation will come about in due course.

A crew from CBC's *The Nature of Things* with David Suzuki made a documentary about Abraham's story, which was broadcast in the fall of 2015. Perhaps that gives some closure to this shameful part of our history.

Fall 2003

Community histories are popular in Newfoundland and Labrador. Although the quality varies, they are usually hodgepodges of genealogy, folk belief, factual material borrowed from secondary sources, family photos, and a few muddy reproductions of rare documents. In many ways, *Hopedale: Three Ages of a Community in Northern Labrador* resembles these rough diamonds, but there is nothing rough about this work. It's a real jewel.

Hopedale is an excellent example of what deep pockets and a trained researcher can do to produce a first-rate community history. The photos, engravings, maps, and art works are beautifully represented in black and white and colour, the documentation is meticulous without being in the least intimidating, and the text is smooth and lucid. Of course, it helps to be able to draw on the resources of a community of religious missionaries who believed in documenting everything they did for over two hundred years.

Brice-Bennett has identified in the history of Hopedale three distinct eras, each distinguished by the place name in use at the time: Arvertok in Inuttitut, the "place of bowhead whales" which was occupied at the earliest period of interaction with European groups; Hoffenthal, or "vale of hope" in German, where the Moravians proselytized and operated a trading post; and Hopedale, the modern community that emerged when the Hudson's Bay Company took over in 1926.

The text of *Hopedale* draws on diaries, extracts from the *Periodical Accounts of the Moravian Missions*, biographies, and various other documents, but most of the text is Brice-Bennett's own distillation of her copious reading and research. It is a little stiff at times, but this is more than compensated for by the lively and colourful illustrations. She has brought together historic engravings, a century or more of photographs, paintings, batiks, and murals, to depict people, artifacts, landscapes, and documents.

The many illustrations give the sense that this is a picture book or a particularly handsome scrapbook, which is not the case. The designer has distinguished between regular chapters and short "window" pieces by laying the latter over a faint engraving of a whale, but this isn't entirely successful. Once you get absorbed by the narrative, it is easy to miss the visual clue and find yourself suddenly reading about a totally different subject. Furthermore, the darker edge of the underlying engraving makes the print harder to read. The small grey print used for identifying the sources of the illustrations is probably intended not to distract from the more important photos and drawings, but for a reader who wants to know where these beautiful images come from, it is a bit of a struggle.

The only real omission in this otherwise admirable book is that of the voices of the people of Hopedale themselves. Yes, we are told what they thought and did, but only in the third person. We get occasional quotations from the Moravian missionaries that give a little insight into the lives and personalities of these Europeans and their families, but there is virtually no direct quotation from any of the people they served. Obviously, it is easier to quote from historic figures who kept diaries, but the oral tradition is still strong in Labrador, and Brice-Bennett has considerable expertise in that area, as is evident in her previous book with Paulus Maggo.

Quibbles aside, *Hopedale* is a lovely book for reading and for browsing. One can only hope that the Historic Sites Association continues to support such comprehensive and attractive work.

The Fur Trade

George Cartwright; Aimee Chaulk; Leonard Budgell; Philip E.L. Smith

JUST as Canada's early history is inextricably associated with the fur trade, so is that of Labrador. Right up until the Second World War, the interior was thought to be good only for trapping. Coastal Labradorians could fish in the summer, and of course thousands of Newfoundlanders went north to fish as well, but there was not much of a living to be made inland except by trappers and the merchants who supplied them and bought their furs. As W.G. Gosling reminds us in his history of Labrador, "the furriers were the pioneers; the genuine fishermen did not arrive until many years later."

He describes the early European traders as "independent men not working for the Hudson's Bay Company, or any particular mercantile concern," men like George Cartwright, although later, there were also the Hudson's Bay Company and other fur trade firms such as Revillon Frères and the Moravian Mission.

One of the most interesting and important books written about Labrador has got to be *A Journal of Transactions and Events on the Coast of Labrador,*

George Cartwright's account of his six journeys to the coast between 1770 and 1786, yet for various reasons it tends to be overlooked in its original form. First of all, it was published in three volumes, making it an expensive purchase. Secondly, it would be a rather lengthy undertaking to read all 1,055 pages. Thirdly, as years have passed, it has become more difficult to find copies. Lastly, Cartwright includes a good deal of information, such as weather and accounts of hunting trips, that tends to be rather repetitive and wearisome.

In time, technology solved the problem of rarity, and I was fortunate to be given a "Reprinted on Demand" copy produced by University Microfilms International when one of my old professors retired. However, I was still challenged by sentences such as "I ſent Charles and Haines to open the Beaverhouſe in Iſland Lake," as well as the repetitions and the sheer length of the work.

Chunks of Cartwright's *Journal* appear in anthologies and are quoted in academic works, and I often found myself going back to that three-volume reprint to check quotations for context, but as Labrador wasn't my area of study at that time, I never sat down and read the entire thing. Then I met Eva Luther in Fox Harbour and discovered that she had indexed all three volumes, and was willing to give me a copy of her index. Suddenly, the *Journal* opened up to me, and those pesky long s's were worth the effort of reading them.

Next I acquired a copy of Marianne Stopp's *New*

Labrador Papers of Captain George Cartwright, which consists of 115 "additions to the *Labrador Companion*" (a book of lessons drawn from the journal, prepared by Cartwright himself and published in 1810) as well as "shorter texts, correspondence, and miscellaneous material on loose sheets," which added another 236 pages of reading to my original 1,055.

Fortunately, I eventually acquired Charles Wendell Townsend's 1911 edited version of the *Journal*, which an introduction by Wilfred Grenfell calls an "accessible edition of those Journals" (p. viii). In the Preface, Townsend claims to have "reproduced the Journal without any changes in the wording, spelling or punctuation," omitting only "much that is of necessity tedious and of little interest to the general reader, and much that is mere repetition." The cover of my copy, a discard from the Fort Garry Public Library, had come away from the bound pages, and the map was torn, but it was legible and a mere 380 pages long. I flew through it in only two days.

What I had searched for and failed to find in my occasional explorations of the original *Journal*, I found in Townsend's edition: storms at sea, pirates, theft, treason, house fires, whippings, fraud, bankruptcy, adultery, and enough twists and turns to fuel a soap opera for decades. It was a wonderful read.

Townsend's version of the *Journal* also contains lots of the stuff of daily life. We learn that Cartwright was a determined gardener, that he had two tame grey jays loose in his house, and that his kitchen caught fire no fewer than four times in one day, because the chimney was made of wood. He preferred to wear linen to flannel, could and would eat just about anything, favouring rank old wolf meat over salt beef or pork. He liked naming hills, ponds, and other geographical locations, and he loved the "sport" of hunting.

For animal lovers, Cartwright's relentless hunting might be a bit off-putting. He killed everything that moved, including not just bears, caribou, geese, and ducks, but also seagulls, mourning doves, and pine grosbeaks. He tended to eat most of these things, or used them for bait for fishing, but even when he had lots of meat on hand, he couldn't see an animal without wanting to shoot it. Once, when butchering two caribou that he'd shot, he stopped to shoot a raven that was perched on a nearby tree, in contrast to the local Innu, who tended to hang the entrails of the animals they killed in the trees for the jays and ravens to feed on. Probably Cartwright's enthusiastic slaughter of polar bears is particularly hard to stomach in the current time, because they are endangered, but even by the standards of his time, it's difficult to find any justification for his killing six of the beasts in one day when none of the meat and only one of the pelts was harvested for human use.

Cartwright was a real bean-counter, a man with the soul of a shopkeeper. He was always tallying the number of ducks he'd shot, eggs he'd collected, fish he'd caught, barrels he'd filled, or skins he'd bought. If he'd killed a pregnant hare, he counted the number of fetuses in her womb. If he killed a stag, he counted the points in its antlers. Yet his obsession with these numbers brings home as nothing else can the fecundity of Labrador at that time, the teeming natural wealth of the place.

Cartwright saw himself as a highly moral man, honest in his dealings with people. When his common-law wife lost a child she had conceived with one of Cartwright's servants, his initial anger eventually dissipated, and his pity induced him to give her an annuity. He did his best to pay off his debts when he lost everything to privateers. It's easy to see him as a profiteer rather than an honest businessman when he trades a tuppence-hapenny comb for a silver fox worth four guineas, but by the standards of his time, he was within his rights. Captain Henry Atkins stopped on the Labrador coast on his way back from a voyage to Davis Strait in 1729, and he traded local people ten shillings of goods for baleen worth 120 pounds sterling. Nobody on either side of the deal lost any sleep over it.

Townsend's edit turns a dunchy tome into an adventure-filled story, vivid and alive with new experiences, exciting discoveries, unusual people, and unfamiliar ways of life. However, glad as I am to have found it, I am just as glad to have the whole original work. I know from my own Arctic travels that there are stretches of tedious, boring, uncomfortable hours to be endured during any adventure, but often those hours are when you learn the most about a person or a place, and sometimes about yourself. One way or another, I know I'll work my way through all three volumes of the *Journal* eventually.

October 2013

When word leaked out in 2013 that *Them Days* was planning a special book-length issue on the Mista-shipu (a.k.a. the Grand River, the Hamilton River, and most recently the Churchill), people interested in or living in Labrador were pleased. When it later emerged that the issue was to be funded by Nalcor Energy, some of the interest turned to distrust. Especially miffed were members of the Grand Riverkeepers, a pressure group opposed to the Lower Churchill hydro development at Muskrat Falls.

As an inaugural subscriber to *Them Days* and a member of the Grand Riverkeepers, I wasn't quite sure what to think of the financial arrangement, but I had faith that *Them Days* editor Aimee Chaulk would find a way to walk the fine line between the two. Nevertheless, when the special issue was finally released, I was pleased to see that there was no obvious bias in the text, and Nalcor's only presence was a two-line acknowledgement and a small logo. If this publication does nothing else, it should show the arts community that it is possible to take big bucks from big business without selling out your ideals and ethics.

Them Days magazine, for those who aren't familiar with it, is an oral history publication that aims to record the history and culture of Labrador in short, easily accessible articles and interviews. At some points in its history, the transcripts used spelled pronunciation, but more recently the editorial board has modified that stand to retain dialect without stooping to the ubiquitous "dis," "dat," "deze," and "doze."

The volume opens with a brief summary of the archaeological record by Scott Neilsen. Neilsen has probably done more varied digs than any other archaeologist in Labrador, partly because he is resident there and can extend his fieldwork beyond the usual six weeks a year, but also because he has made it his business to get to know the Indigenous people of the area and to draw on them for assistance. They learn archaeology and Neilsen learns elements of their culture that give him insight into the material he finds.

Neilsen is the first of numerous commentators to remind readers that the Mista-shipu is not the same river it was 7500 years ago, or even 75 years ago. During what archaeologists call the Early Period of habitation, Muskrat Falls did not exist "because the land had sunk due to the weight of the glaciers and was inundated by water from Hamilton Inlet." More recently, as Joe Goudie realized when he went on the river with his brother Horace in 1989, "the water levels had dropped fourteen feet" since Horace travelled it prior to hydro development.

Much of this special issue is dedicated to the lives

of the trappers who used the river as a highway. The Height-of-Landers, who were the trapping elite of the 1930s, used to travel hundreds of miles upstream to their paths, poling, lining, and hauling their supplies up past Churchill Falls and then reversing the trip with their furs twice a season. Many of the trappers were responsible for guiding and supporting the early geologists and explorers who mapped the backcountry, and later they helped build Goose air base, open up the IOC mines, and construct Churchill Falls hydro. Without them and their knowledge of the river and the country around it, these enormous undertakings might never have been accomplished.

Although they are touched on only lightly, there are hints throughout the articles and interviews with the old timers of some of the myths and legends that are part of the cultural landscape of Labrador. The Traverspine yeti, the sound of Peggy's Note, which could provoke a free-for-all among the trappers, German submarine lore, and an aberrant lead goose—"a big old gander"—all get passing mention. For a more focused account of the last decades of trapping life, readers can always go to *I Never Knowed it Was Hard: Memoirs of a Labrador Trapper* by Louie Montague.

Some of these trappers were only fourteen years old when they began travelling the river, so it is no surprise that after being alone in the bush for months at a time, they sometimes got a bit spooked. Brian Michelin once came back to his tilt to find the frozen body of an Innu Elder put inside for safekeeping. He hoisted her onto his fur platform for the duration of his stay and then replaced her in the cabin to await burial by her family when he left.

Both Harry Mitsuk and Vera Butt describe the overt racism that was practiced in the early days of settlement of Happy Valley. Harry is a Nunatsiavut beneficiary and Vera is NunatuKavummiut. Both recall that when their families moved to Goose Bay to get work on the Base, a self-appointed committee forbade them to settle on the mainland, but forced them out to Eskimo Island and John White's Island, just offshore. "We wasn't allowed to build on this side see, not Eskimos," is how Harry put it. Vera recalls that when they first arrived, "when we went to set up the tent, Mr. Perrault said we couldn't because Dad wasn't working and there was no land we could put a tent on."

Mitsuk and Butt were young enough to adjust to life on the tiny islands in the river, but it was hard for their fathers, who had to travel over rotten ice in the spring and fall to get to work at the Base. When Harry was old enough to go looking for work on the Valley side, he fell through the ice and almost drowned.

The last page of *The Grand River/Mista-shipu* is a foldout map of the river with prominent areas numbered and listed. I canoed the river some years ago with Elizabeth and Francis Penashue, but we had no maps nor any English names for the feeder rivers and landmarks. It was fascinating to read this volume and put *akenashau* names and histories to the

Innu places I was introduced to on that trip.

What finally comes through from this special issue is the unease felt by those most familiar with the river about the effect that the Muskrat Falls hydro project will have on the ecosystem. These are not hysterical voices of protest. They are thoughtful, nostalgic, knowledgeable, concerned men and women who have lived hard lives but who know the value of clean air and water, and who hope to leave some undisturbed country to their grandchildren. That's not a lot to ask, considering how much they have given and lost.

January 2010

One man who would have lamented the changes in the Churchill River was fur trader Leonard Budgell. Despite the subtitle, *Arctic Twilight: Leonard Budgell and Canada's Changing North* is not a book about him—it is a book by him. Only the last twenty-five pages, an odd compendium of sources, index, service record, biography, and (most odd of all) an interview with the editor, does not come directly from several thousand pages of letters written by Budgell himself.

Leonard Budgell was a Labrador man, born in North West River and raised mostly in Rigolet, who except for a brief spell in the armed forces, spent his life in service to the Hudson's Bay Company. Budgell was one of a number of Labradorians who made careers further north, including Ernie Lyall, John, George, and William Ford, as well as others.

The Labrador men recruited into the HBC were generally more successful than their colleagues from Scotland, because they spoke at least some Inuttitut and had a basic education in living the trapping life. Like most Hudson's Bay servants, they also understood the value of keeping post and personal diaries and recording their experiences on paper. Quite a few of them have left us written accounts of their lives.

Budgell's version of northern life differs from those of many of the Hudson's Bay traders in that he was a born naturalist with a philosophical bent. He had plenty of tales of adventure and he tells quite a few of them here, but his writing has more in common with Newfoundland artist Gary Saunders than with Ernie Lyall. Budgell enjoyed his adventures, but clearly the majority of his life's pleasures came from observations of nature, association with children (particularly his own), and the companionship of true friends.

It's hard to put a finger on exactly what it is about Budgell's writing that is so appealing, because it is generally simple and straightforward, but perhaps it is the sheer joy he finds in remembering. A trip into the country with his brother, when they found a lake they had never seen before, took place in thirty below weather, yet he recalls being warm and well fed and happy. Brief glimpses of wildlife, the taste of fresh brook trout, and a warm fire at the end of a long day elicit almost as much pleasure when recalled fifty years later as they did when he experienced them in his youth. Here is a man with a Wordsworthian sense of the sublime.

There are passages of pure whimsy in this book, too, that will help even the city dweller grow closer to nature. Montreal is described as being like "a lovely woman cleaning an old-fashioned stove, and the soot gets on her face and in her hair." By April she will have washed and changed her dress and "she'll be so radiant that all the people will smile and feel that winter can never come again." While attending a meeting, he looks down twenty-six stories at a little church below: "She sits there, and the big buildings crowd in on her and she draws her skirts back" because they have stolen her sunlight and her view.

There is also, of course, an enormous amount to be learned about Labrador and the north from the pages of this book, but *caveat emptor*. Readers should keep in mind that the work was published posthumously and did not have the benefit of Budgell's proofreading. There are some blatant geographical errors that likely originated with the editor, at least one of the photos is reversed or mislabeled, and I noted over thirty significant typographical errors, which means there were probably more than sixty.

Otherwise, the book is absolutely beautifully produced, with a sturdy and attractive binding, a perfectly gorgeous paper cover, and clear and generous typesetting and layout. What a pity about the errors, because this is a book that deserves not just reading, but rereading.

Philip E.L. Smith's *In Quest of Fur: The Travel Journal of William O.K. Ross, 1909*, from the Creative Book Publishing imprint, could not be more different from Leonard Budgell's *Arctic Twilight*, but it teaches a lesson in history, and it is a model of research. Remarkably little is known about the fur buyers who traveled into Labrador from Quebec, and yet they played an important part in keeping prices competitive. The recently released diary of Rev. Henry Gordon mentions Dave Borenstein from Montreal, who was buying furs in 1919, and people in Labrador remember Frank Bannikhin, who expanded from buying furs and eventually had over two dozen herring factories on the Labrador and Newfoundland coasts, but there were dozens of other fur buyers travelling in the area who came and went without any record.

In Quest of Fur consists of a 30-page transcript of diary entries by a Quebec City fur buyer as he traveled by foot, dogteam, and boat through Labrador and into the Northern Peninsula of Newfoundland, and 145 pages of introduction, endnotes, and bibliography by Smith.

A proportion of five pages of documentation to one page of text may seem too great for the average reader, but for the historian or genealogist, it is about right. Smith shows just how much background labour goes into even the simplest research project. He tracks down almost every person mentioned in the diary, gives as much background information about them as he can, briefly outlines the history of each of the communities Ross visited, sorts out variant spellings and conflicting information, and in general, tries to make sense of the brief but compelling diary entries.

In Quest of Fur is the first serious study of the independent fur-buying industry in Labrador, and it is a gem that will be read, savoured and cherished by amateur enthusiasts and professional historians alike.

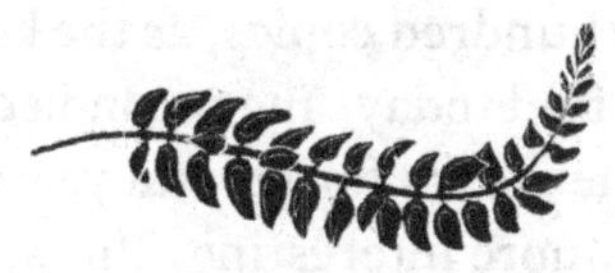

Miscellany

Them Days; John Gimlette;
Kenn Harper; Lawrence Millman;
John C. Kennedy; Phillip Igloliorti

June 2010

SNOWBLIND and Seal Finger, a book about early medicine in Labrador, was first published in 1998 as a small supplement to *Them Days* magazine. That first and only print run must have been very small, perhaps a few hundred copies, as the book is almost impossible to find today. The second edition, which has been in the works for several years, is twice as long and even more interesting. This second edition divides the material into categories, including the history of medicine on the Labrador coast, home remedies, accidents, childbirth, dentistry, mental health, epidemics, nursing, and visits from the doctor.

The home remedies seem to attract the most attention from readers, probably because of how strange some of them are. Everyone of a certain age remembers having their heads doused with kerosene for lice, or having bread poultices applied to boils, not to mention being dosed with Friar's Balsam and

Vick's VapoRub, or being painted like a Van Gogh sunset with iodine, mercurochrome, gentian violet, and other startling concoctions. However, have you ever had a fresh mouse skin applied to warts or the guts of a fish rubbed into your back? Probably not.

The section on childbirth and midwifery will be of interest now that the practice of natural childbirth and home delivery is making a return. But to have these things without the safety net of a nearby hospital must have been nerve-wracking indeed.

Two new additions to the second edition make a real contribution to the history of medical practice in this area. Innu advocate Makkus Penashue describes how he builds and operates sweatlodges for healing both mental and physical ailments, and former Grenfell nurse Susan Felsberg outlines the daily duties of a station nurse serving a large, isolated community.

Another welcome addition to this new and expanded history of health in Labrador is extracts from the diary of Arthur and Marjorie Wakefield. The Wakefields were, respectively, a doctor and a social worker with the Grenfell Mission. They served for many years, and during World War I they became organizers of the Legion of Frontiersmen, which provided many Labrador recruits for the Newfoundland Regiment.

Snowblind and Seal Finger gives only a taste of what can be found in the *Them Days* archive, but the last page lists two dozen other articles on related subjects that can be read in back issues of the magazine.

Although some of the photos reproduced here are a bit dark, and the proofreading is disappointingly casual, this is a fascinating little book that will appeal to history buffs and those old enough to remember when folk medicine was all there was to rely on.

March 2005

In 1893, a young medical missionary named Eliot Curwen travelled to Labrador to work with Wilfred Grenfell for a few months. He stopped in St. John's on his way up the coast, dined with the Governor, traveled on to Battle Harbour where he treated over a thousand patients, and made his way home to England after an aborted visit to the French Shore.

By the time Curwen had finished his brief Labrador stint, he'd had enough of Labrador and Grenfell. He took himself off to China for six years, got the wandering bug out of his system, and settled in as a country doctor in Sussex, where he wrote a number of important books on Neolithic culture. His Labrador photographs were inherited by his granddaughter, his Inuit artifacts went to the British Museum, and that was that until 1999, when Ron Rompkey published some of Curwen's diaries under the title *Labrador Odyssey*.

While we can thank Rompkey for giving us access to Curwen's wonderful photographs and absorbing diary entries, we may want to blame him for attracting the attention of Curwen's great-grandson, John Gimlette, author of *Theatre of Fish: Travels Through Newfoundland and Labrador*. Newfoundland and Labrador didn't really need another kick at the Annie Proulx cat, but that's about what it got, dressed up this time as non-fiction.

I confess, I was initially rather taken with this irreverent history masquerading as a travel book, but by the time I had ploughed half-way through, the gross errors, crude stereotypes, and literary strip-mining had lost their charm. It reminded me of a wine-soaked dinner party I attended that was so much fun, we decided to do it all again the next evening. Big mistake.

As a boy, John Gimlette attended Mostyn House School, once the Grenfell family home and in Gimlette's time run by Sir Wilfred's great-nephew. He had what he calls a "well-Grenfelled childhood," and curious about the unfinished saga of his great-grandfather's truncated involvement with the mission, he set out over a hundred years later to retrace his journey.

Gimlette is a man of excesses, a fact that will be evident to any perceptive reader by page 3 of his narrative, when he explains that in Newfoundland, "Cod was, literally, king." Well, no, it wasn't literally king, it was metaphorically king, but such subtleties mean little to Gimlette, who borrows from Hammond Innes and Wayne Johnston as liberally as he does from Prowse, Horwood, Howley, Smallwood, and Ingstad.

The book opens in St. John's, at a bar on Water Street where an Australian stripper is sliding down a pole to shouts of "God love ya, me old trout." Why not? There are, heaven knows, enough bars in St. John's, and a few of them have strippers. Surely it's as legitimate a place to begin as a library or an art gallery. The trouble is, we never seem to get out of the bar.

Gimlette's Newfoundland is peopled primarily by poachers, boozers, scam-artists, half-wits, and brutalized women, and Gimlette's Labrador is much the same, except that the IQs are lower and the rum intake higher. I have only to shake the family tree to locate a few half-wit inebriates in my own immediate circle, but that doesn't mean that's all there is to this place.

He doesn't get it all wrong, of course. He catches Janet Story perfectly, and has lots of fun with his take on John Crosbie, whom he refers to as the Minister of Fish throughout. His understanding of the outport dramas put on for tourists, "digging away at the interstices between Newfoundland's pride and its self-loathing," is insightful. But most of the time he keeps very bad company and never attracts the attention of anyone willing or able to take the time to set him straight on anything.

The author plunders dozens of other people's books—everything from history to exploration to travel-writing—for gossip, scandal, and curiosities to entertain his readers, and he's obviously dipped into the *Dictionary of Newfoundland English*, scattering dialect words randomly throughout the province with no apparent awareness that many of these are regionally restricted, and generally has a brawling, bawdy, utterly un-Grenfellian time doing it. But it gets tiresome.

It's inevitable that some factual errors will slip by Gimlette, but I noted several dozen glaring ones before I gave up counting. And surely he doesn't really believe that the Ingstads spent their lives constructing an elaborately fake archeological site. His comments about the costal boat's visit to Davis Inlet say a great deal about the deckhands' racism but nothing whatsoever about the Mushuau Innu he has never even met. His supposed insight into the citizens of Nain, gained from graffiti which he renders as "SMASHIN BUMPKINS," might have been revised had he known that Smashing Pumpkins is a rock group.

John Gimlette is only out for a bit of fun, so what harm is there in his twisted rendering of our history and the conditions of our lives today? Ask Margaret Wente. She described Newfoundland as a "vast and scenic welfare ghetto," full of "ingrates on pogey," and got two thousand emails outlining Newfoundlanders' thoughts on the subject. Gimlette has already had more hours of my time than he deserves.

*

Winter 2017-18

Linguist and historian Kenn Harper is well known throughout the North as the author of numerous columns in the *Nunatsiaq News*, two collections of essays on Arctic history, and the best-seller *Give Me My Father's Body*, now revised and available as *Minik: The New York Eskimo*. Fluent in Inuktitut, Harper has access to information denied to most historians, and he makes good use of it. In recent years, Harper has turned his attention more frequently toward Newfoundland and Labrador, contributing articles to publications such as *Them Days* and *Labrador Life*. His most recent book, *Thou Shalt Do No Murder: Inuit, Injustice, and the Canadian Arctic*, is not directly about Labrador, but many of the players who appear in its pages have Labrador connections, including Moses, George, and John Bartlett of Turnavik West; Ralph Parsons of the Hudson's Bay Company; Inuit interpreter James Tooktoshina; and the body in the case, trader Robert Janes.

In mid-March of 1920, an Inuk leader known as Nuqallaq shot and killed Janes at a camp in North Baffin known in English as Cape Crauford. It took three years for the police to learn of the killing, investigate the circumstances, establish a temporary court at Pond Inlet, and bring Nuqallaq to trial. Two other Inuit were implicated and charged in the apparent murder. One was acquitted, and the other was found guilty of manslaughter with a recommendation for clemency, but Nuqallaq's manslaughter conviction earned him 10 years imprisonment with hard labour.

The background of the killing was that Janes was one of three free traders working the Pond Inlet area, the others being Jamie Florence, representing Henry Toke Munn, and Wilfred Caron, representing Capt. Joseph-Elzéar Bernier. Competition was fierce among the three, and because of bad ice conditions and a lack of cooperation, Janes found himself stranded in Baffin for four years with supplies for only two.

As Janes had less and less to trade or even to feed himself, he became more unstable and began threatening to shoot people, or to shoot their dogs, which would have condemned the entire group to death by starvation. As anthropologist Jean Briggs has argued, in Inuit tradition, "Expressions of ill temper towards human beings . . . are never considered justified in anyone over the age of three or four." Janes was thought to be seriously out of control and a danger to everyone around him.

Language issues played a large part in Nuqallaq's trial. Munn, who inserted himself into the investigation, spoke English but only halting Inuktitut; five of the six jury members spoke only French and none spoke Inuktitut; Duval, the official interpreter, spoke fluent Inuktitut and English but no French, so the Crown Prosecutor had to interpret for the jury; and finally the police interpreter Tooktoshina spoke English but no French, and his Labrador dialect led to frequent errors of translation.

According to the sources Harper consulted, the

Inuit believed that it was necessary to their own survival that Janes, whom they thought had "lost his mind from homesickness," be eliminated. According to his rival Munn and Staff Sergeant Alfred Joy, who led the investigation, the killing was motivated by jealousy over a woman both Janes and Nuqallaq had been involved with some years before, although there was little actual evidence to support this contention. As for the motivation of the Canadian justice system, Harper argues quite convincingly that the pursuit of the Janes case was prompted not by respect for the principles of justice, but by a desire to establish Canadian sovereignty in North Baffin. Nuqallaq, predictably, contracted tuberculosis after two years in Stony Mountain Penitentiary in Manitoba before he was sent home to die.

Thou Shalt Do No Murder tells a complex and exciting story that contains real insight into traditional Inuit life, and it should be required reading for every teacher, social worker and justice worker in Labrador. An enormous amount of what Harper has to say about the Canadian justice system almost a century ago is still relevant today.

March 2005

When I see the word "retold" on the title page of a book, my guard usually goes up, because I am sure that someone has been at work with a censor's pencil, bowdlerizing the text. I'm also a little skeptical about Lawrence Millman as an authority on Northern matters, as he has gotten things wrong in previous books. I heard him lecture at the Labrador Interpretation Centre some years ago, and when audience members pointed out errors of fact, he ignored them and blithely carried on miseducating them about their own environment.

Despite my skepticism, I think he got some things right in one curious little book. *Wolverine the Trickster: Labrador Innu Tales* is a collection of twenty short Innu stories about the mythic figure of Wolverine. Such stories would probably be categorized by most librarians as fiction, but for the Innu, they are as true and as important as the stories found in the Bible. Considering the content of most of the Innu trickster tales, such a comparison might seem blasphemous, but as editor Millman points out, Innu-aimun references to genitalia and bodily functions "carry no moral or immoral connotations whatsoever." Virtually all these stories are scatological or contain what day time talk-shows coyly call "potty talk," so if that makes you uneasy, give this small volume a miss.

If, on the other hand, you have heard the words "shit" and "fart" before, and you have a hankering to know what Innu find interesting and funny, *Wolverine the Trickster* might be a good start.

Wolverine is the Labrador manifestation of Wile E. Coyote and Roadrunner rolled into one, pulling off crazy stunts one minute and being humiliated and bested the next. He can sweet-talk anybody into handing over a good meal or a comely wife, he has a monstrous appetite and a private appendage of monumental proportions, and he can fart to beat the band.

Do Innu really love fart jokes, and can they really use those rude noises to foretell the future? Yes, gentle reader, they can and they do, and once you've spent a week or two in close company with these people, you will start to realize that your own European attitudes towards that function are a bit... well, "anal" is the only word that comes to mind.

Millman, like many story tellers, goes a bit over the top at times. I very much doubt that Thomas Pastitshi was actively tubercular in the 1980s, and if there was a shaking tent ceremony in Sheshatshiu in 1988, it's still a well-kept secret locally. However, much of what he says about the European bowdlerization of Indigenous stories is true, and he's to be commended for refusing to bend to such hypocrisy. *Wolverine the Trickster* provides a good opportunity to see a side of the Innu culture that you won't find on the evening news, a side that is funnier and, in many ways, more true.

Spring 2016

Although author John C. Kennedy refers to his new book, *Encounters: An Anthropological History of Southeastern Labrador*, as a revision of his earlier work, *People of the Bays and Headlands*, it is really a new book, containing information and insights that twenty or thirty years ago were not thought of. *Encounters* covers all the history of the Labrador coast from Chateau Bay to north of Sandwich Bay, beginning with the archaeological record, through the ethnohistory, ethnography, and genealogy of the area. It is a broad, dense, and complex look at a large geographical region with a relatively small population, currently consisting of eleven communities, each with a mere handful of people.

It has been argued by many, including the Canadian and Newfoundland governments, that southeastern Labrador was never an Inuit area, and that the people there have no land claims or Indigenous rights. Kennedy proves that this is incorrect. By government decree, most of the Inuit in southern Labrador were deliberately pushed towards the north, in order to leave the coast clear for European fishers. They were also coaxed and lured north by the presence of Moravian missionaries with access to trade goods and medicine, and actively discouraged from remaining in their traditional regions.

However, some Inuit remained in the southeastern areas, and many eventually intermarried with European immigrants. As Kennedy makes clear, however, "the real difference between historic Inuit in northern and southeastern Labrador was the Moravians." Despite Christianization and the suppression of many traditional practices by the Moravians, a clearly Inuit culture survived in the north, while numerous Inuit south of Lake Melville "succumbed to alcohol, disease or assimilation."

Individuals who resent benefits being extended to those of mixed heritage in southeastern Labrador mockingly insist that nobody from the region was anxious to claim Native heritage until there was something in it for them. There is some truth to that suggestion. Why set out to prove that you are a second-class citizen, unable to vote, discriminated against, tormented and bullied at school, when you can keep your mouth shut and be judged by what you do rather than who your grandmother was?

Jewish men who emigrated to Newfoundland from England and intermarried with the Christian population often suppressed, denied, or even forgot their cultural heritage, because by Jewish law, their children were not Jews. By Canadian law, however, people with Inuit or Innu grandparents were Indigenous and had a right to benefits that were subsequently denied to them. Once the stigma of Indigenous ancestry was removed, they had every reason to assert their claim and to celebrate what had once been a source of pain and discrimination.

Parts of this book are a bit too detailed for the general reader, but they are necessary for the proper telling of what amounts to a new story, and even the boring bits deserve attention. As with the Bible, there are a lot of "begats," and if you aren't a descendent of a begat yourself, it is hard to stay involved. However, being told that Jephtha or Job or Rachel had lots of descendants is simply not the same as having those children and grandchildren named and married off, employed, and buried. Kennedy goes beyond simple genealogy and tells the stories of these families.

Compiling a history of any area of Labrador is difficult, because there is little objective documentation. The missionaries tended to stress moral weakness in their parishioners to highlight the need for Christian values of industry and observance; those associated with the Grenfell Mission often exaggerated poverty and disease for fundraising purposes; traders had the bottom line to consider and were often justifying profits and losses to owners geographically far removed from the situation; and even the few government representatives present, such as magistrates and policing agencies, often had personal agendas that shaped how they presented facts and figures.

Kennedy is well aware of all these factors and does his best to balance these disparate records. Just as importantly, he warns his readers when he is speculating on thin or unreliable evidence. Perhaps, this book being a revision of an earlier work, he learned along the way how fallible the historian sometimes can be.

One disappointing but not surprising aspect of *Encounters* is that Kennedy adheres to the anthropological custom of not naming living informants. The deceased are identified, but if he is recounting the experience of people still alive, they become anonymous Joes or Janes, whether they wish to or not. No doubt the people in some of the smaller communities have no trouble identifying the Joes and Janes, but the larger readership will have to be satisfied with pseudonyms, and that is a pity, because the individuals behind those names sound like fascinating people with lots to say for themselves.

While *Encounters* will be of special interest to the people of southeastern Labrador and their relatives, readers with an interest in many disparate subjects will also find a lot to enjoy in this book. There is much fresh information about the judges, magistrates, and the justice system; the merchants and coasting traders; the explorers and entrepreneurs; the medical, educational, and religious missionaries; government bureaucrats; the Newfoundland Rangers; resettled communities; the herring, whaling, and trapping industries, and of course the cod fishery.

There is an old joke about the visitor to Labrador who, after a day, writes an article about the place, and after a week, writes a book. It takes an honest and determined investigator to come back year after year, for literally decades, to search for the truth and to set the record straight. Georg Henriksen did just that for the Innu of the Northern Labrador coast, but he was one of a small and select group. John C. Kennedy can now add his name to that list of honest and respected academics who have dedicated their working lives to documenting the history of the people of Labrador.

Fall 2000

A century ago, Inuit had the reputation of being among the best pre-literate poets known to the Western world. There was a certain irony in the fact that Inuit poetry was lauded only after it had almost ceased to exist, but the interest that collectors such as Knud Rasmussen, Svend Frederiksen and, later, John Robert Colombo stimulated in the old spontaneous compositions convinced people that literature does not have to be written to be worthy of the name. Phillip Igloliorti goes a step further and demonstrates in his first full-length poetry collection, *I Hope It Don't Rain Tonight,* that literature does not even have to be literary to be worthy of the name. This observation is offered without malice. Igloliorti's poetry, when judged by the usual standards of such work in English, is lamentable, yet it has a power and an impact that makes it interesting and at times even compelling reading.

Traditional Inuit poems were loosely categorized by Rasmussen as songs of mood, hunting songs, chants and incantations, and songs of derision. Modern Inuit poetry tends to fit into similar divisions, although hunting songs have evolved into poems heavy with political content, and charms or chants have been adapted to accommodate Christianity. The ability to develop close personal relationships outside the family has accrued considerable importance in post-contact Inuit life, with the result that modern Inuit poetry now tends to focus on romantic love rather than sex or marriage, but pensive songs of mood are still being written, as are satirical songs of derision.

Phillip Igloliorti fits easily into the pattern of forms and content that can be found by Inuit poets and musicians elsewhere in Canada. Like Mary Panegoosho and Charlie Panegoniak, he sometimes composes short, reflective works that are almost imagistic in their approach, but like most of the younger poets, typified by Alootook Ipellie, he uses poetic conventions, including rhyme and metre, better suited to English than to Inuktitut.

Igloliorti's experiments in English poetics are not a success. Consider the following opening verses of three poems chosen at random: "My mother dear, / I love you dear / my waterfall of tears / is filled"; "I cry my tears / in rains that fall / hiding the pain / that is never small"; and "We sometimes fight, / resolve with a kiss, / ignoring at times / what I have to fix." Throughout the book, his rhyme is not just inexact, but downright discordant. The grating near-misses are made worse by an adherence to rhyme schemes that are only consistent enough to allow for betrayal. He is also like the man whose limericks never would scan, because he always "tries to put as many words into the last line as he possibly can." Add to that bad grammar (as distinct from dialect, such as can be found in the title of the book), muddy logic, and what even Séamus Ó Ceallaigh, who wrote the introduction to the collection, calls "cliché" and the "linguistic relics of pop culture" and you have some very bad poetry indeed.

If this were all that could be said about Iglolior-ti's work, there would be little reason to waste more printer's ink discussing it, but it is impossible for this reader to dismiss the gut-wrenching content. Some of the poems are about sexual abuse, and many more are about the loneliness and isolation that inevitably follow a childhood full of physical and emotional terror. If the child survivors of the infamous Terezin concentration camp wrote poetry, this is what it might be like.

One hundred years ago, explicit sex was a common subject in Inuit poetry. When the poet Netsit discussed men's impotence, he was not just being metaphorical. And neither the unidentified man who composed the song of longing for Analuk's wife nor the singer Kibkarjuk who accused Utahania of desiring his own younger sister held back on the details of these desires. Even the hunting songs of the old Inuit poets were often overtly sexual. Yet sixty years ago, when Inuit poetry written in English began to appear, sexual matters were avoided. By the late 1960s, one did not encounter anything remotely like the blunt treatment of sexuality that the traditional Inuit poets produced.

This book breaks that missionary-imposed taboo. Sex in Igloliorti's poetry is raw, painful, confused, and as likely to lead to anger as to fulfillment. As a survivor of child sexual abuse, he is torn between the imposed homosexual experiences that he both endured and desired, and the heterosexual love that has given him a wife and child he adores. The anger and confusion that results from these dichotomies are expressed in terms of natural phenomena such as tornadoes, avalanches and waterfalls. One of the better poems that uses such a metaphor is "Exhausted Trees," in which trees covered in glitter are so weighed down by the ice that they are suicidal. Throughout the poems, the only erotic touch the poet really enjoys is wind on his skin, a sensation that is safe, distant, removed from human contact. The longing for security and the inability to endure closeness is heartbreaking.

Obviously, Phillip Igloliorti's poetry is a form of therapy for him, and it would probably be very useful in treating other survivors of child abuse, but that isn't the purpose of poetry. Poetry may heal, but if it is written for that purpose, it usually fails as poetry. Igloliorti clearly believes he is writing something that has poetic value or he might have simply gone on *Oprah* or written a tell-all autobiography. His intent is evident in the very forms he chooses to use and fails to use successfully.

There is probably not a person in Canada today who does not recognize that a collection of words in iambic tetrameter with an ABAB rhyme scheme is in some way poetic. The dozens of nursery rhymes, ballads, and popular songs that bubble up out of the memories of unliterary or even illiterate people are most often in that form, or one similar. Possibly Igloliorti wishes to put his feelings and thoughts into a shape that he and others recognize as poetry, because sometimes those feelings and thoughts are simply too important to be contained in anything common or prosaic.

Igloliorti is not alone in his desire to use familiar English poetic forms of rhyme and metre to elevate his thoughts. Labrador writers such as Bob Palliser, Christine Poker, and Rose Gregoire, not to mention numerous young unpublished Labrador writers, all choose rhyme and metre rather than the less restrictive free verse. The reason such writers choose a verse form that even skilled first-language English speakers find difficult to use is unclear. Perhaps to the writer for whom English is not the mother-tongue (even if it is the only language the writer speaks), deep and bleak, soul and gold, sound the same. Perhaps the fractured scansion sounds fine to writers who come from a tradition where a song may be in 3-4 time and the drum that accompanies it may be in 2-4, or notes are deliberately flattened or sharpened so that they seem incorrect to the Western ear. Possibly these writers are using the only forms they are sure will be accepted as poetic by the dominant society.

The answer to the puzzle of contemporary Indigenous poetry is education. Writers must be educated so that when they fracture a rhyme scheme or a line length, they are doing it to some purpose, and readers must be educated so that they are open to new poetic forms and devices that may be borrowed from older Indigenous traditions, or invented to accommodate new ones. In the meantime, Igloliorti's *I Hope It Don't Rain Tonight* provides readers with a glimpse into the mind of at least one of the many Indigenous people who have managed to wrest some artistic satisfaction out of a language they speak by default, a tradition that mocked their own, and a culture that appropriated their voices and denied them validity. Broken Jaw Press took a great chance when it decided to publish these poems, but it was the right decision, and I have no doubt that Philip Igloliorti's next book will be better, because he has the courage and a fierce need to be heard. He deserves an audience.

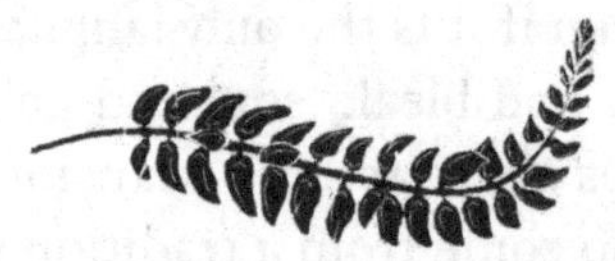

The Diarist Tradition

2015

DIARIES, or letters kept in diary style, were among the first literary forms to be employed by Indigenous people in Labrador and elsewhere in the Canadian north. They were adopted from at least three European models: the ship's log, the trading post journal, and religious mission records. The original manuscripts rarely survived, because paper was always needed to provide wadding for shotgun shells, and converts were forbidden to tear pages out of prayer books and Bibles. Translations appeared in print, and enough examples of original diaries eventually made their way into archives to establish that Inuit diaries and letters were not anomalies in the nineteenth and twentieth centuries. The diary was a convenient method of presenting everyday situations and events, and was probably popular because it was immediate, personal, and so flexible in form, based on autobiographies, memoirs, journals, letters, or a mixture of all these things.

There were certain limits as to what was considered appropriate subject matter for autobiographical works, but as Inuit intermarried with people of European descent, the diary tradition became more embedded, so that numerous members of one family were all keeping, and eventually publishing, diaries. Such was the case with Lydia Campbell, her daughter Margaret Baikie, her grandson Thomas Blake, and her great-grand niece Elizabeth Goudie.

Added to the diarist tradition was a proliferation of Inuit language or bilingual periodicals that were published by or for Labrador Inuit, including *Aglait Illunainortut* in the 19th century, *Naimuik* in the early 1900s, and *Moraviamiut Labradorime* and *kinatuinamot illengajuk* in the 1970s. Other provincial and national magazines, including *Decks Awash* and *Inuit Today*, sometimes published work by Labrador Inuit writers as well, and *Inuktitut* magazine, out of Ottawa, was edited by Labrador Inuk Sam Metcalfe for many years.

This multitude of manuscripts and published material by Labrador Inuit makes it appear that the literary tradition was and is growing slowly but steadily in Labrador. This impression would be not so much wrong as incomplete, for there are two Indigenous cultures in Labrador. Labrador is home not just to the Inuit and their intermarried relatives, but also to the Mushuau and Sheshatshiu Innu, part of the Algonquian family of First Nations people, who were formerly referred to in English as Montagnais and Naskapi.

Today the Innu of Labrador are becoming increasingly well-known because of their political activism and their fight against the alcohol and drug addictions that came to dominate their lives in the latter half of the twentieth century. However, for much of their recent history, they have been invisible citizens in the former country of Newfoundland, and now Canada. Pencilled out of the Confederation agreement of 1949, denied Indigenous status by the federal government, neglected by the politicians who might have represented them, and dominated by a religious institution that did not encourage self-government, the Innu had no public voice, literary or otherwise, until relatively recently.

While it can be and has been argued by scholars that traditional Inuit culture displayed a natural predisposition towards literacy, which contributed to the almost 100% literacy rates that existed among that group until fairly recently, the same is rarely said about the Innu. However, as speakers of Innu-aimun, part of the Cree language family, one might expect Innu to have embraced literacy (and literature) at the same rate as the Inuit. John Murdoch, a specialist in the spread of syllabics among Indigenous people, has proven that by the 1840s, "as a result of the innovation by James Evans, a Wesleyan Methodist missionary and fluent speaker of the Ojibway Indian language, thousands of Algonquian and Athapaskan Indians were literate [within a decade] without any schooling at all."

Syllabics, a simple system of writing that can be learned in a matter of hours, was easy for nomads to learn—the symbols were simply matched up on a syllabarium written on a bit of wood or birch bark with pictographs reminding the learner of how that syllable sounded. The symbol for "wa" might be accompanied by a pictograph of a rabbit, for *wabush*, while a picture of a *pipitsheu* or robin would accompany the syllabic for the syllable "pi." The syllabic system of writing is still in use among the majority of Ojibway and Cree nations, as well as the Inuit of the Eastern Arctic, with the exception of Labrador. In Labrador, both the Innu and the Inuit use the Roman orthography, the Inuit version introduced by the Moravian missionaries in the late 1700s, and the Innu version promoted by Roman Catholic priests at a somewhat later date.

According to Egerton Young, it is widely believed that syllabics were developed by the Ojibway with the assistance of Rev. Evans when the Hudson's Bay Company refused to transport a printing press for Evans that had been offered to him by the British Wesleyan Conference, forcing him to devise a simpler writing system that he carved out of the lead lining of tea chests and printed using a fur press. The Moravian Brethren of Labrador, however, had their own ships and were easily able to bring a printing press to Nain from Greenland. This allowed them to use a conventional alphabet, which was easier for them to print but more difficult for readers to learn. Despite that, the Inuit of Labrador did become literate and very quickly began writing about themselves, while the Innu did not.

The reasons for the difference in the literary output of these two disparate groups are complex. Some of it might have to do with the linguistic nature of Inuttitut as opposed to that of Innu-aimun, but as Inuttitut is agglutinative and Innu-aimun is, loosely speaking, polysynthetic, which is probably next to agglutinative if languages are on a continuum, the difference is more likely the result of geography, religion and politics. The Inuit of Labrador were lured, coaxed and even compelled into settling on the Labrador coast at a relatively early date. The Moravians wanted their converts to be independent, but they also wanted them to live in stable communities, so they took various steps to ensure that the Inuit gave up their nomadic lifestyle. They employed Inuit in their gardens, provided them with nets for fishing seal and cod, supplied traps and traded furs for European goods, and rewarded them for regular attendance at church. The Moravians did all this without attempting to eliminate their language or kidnap their children. The Christianization of the Labrador Inuit was not without its stresses and pressures, but compared to the Indigenous experiences elsewhere, it was driven by a carrot, not a stick, and the change was accomplished well before the beginning of the twentieth century.

In contrast, the majority of the Innu did not settle in permanent villages in Labrador until the 1960s, after the development of the Upper Churchill flooded much of their traditional hunting grounds. It took many months in a formal classroom for most people to learn to read using the Roman orthography, and the Innu simply did not have—or want—access to those classrooms. A few children attended school in the villages that were founded at Davis Inlet and North West River, but attendance was sporadic and the language barriers considerable since the teachers spoke only English. Syllabics, which was primarily self-taught, could easily have been learned from the Ojibway and Cree to the west, but it made no inroads among the Innu, even in the absence of the formal religion-driven education and printing presses that could be found among the neighbouring Inuit.

During the nineteenth and twentieth century, the Innu of Labrador converted to the Roman Catholic faith, so they came under the influence of the Catholic church rather than that of the Methodists, Anglicans, or Moravians. The nature of the Roman Catholic church virtually guaranteed that literacy was not given a high priority. Reading the Bible was never greatly encouraged in the Catholic education system, where far more emphasis is given to ritual and the sacraments, and until relatively recently, laity were not encouraged to take on active roles in the church. The mission you belonged to influenced where you traded, where and whether your children attended school, whether the second language you might learn would be English or French, and whom you might marry. Even if the conversion was relatively superficial, which it often was right up into the 1920s and beyond, Innu were Roman Catholics socially even if not by conviction. To be Indigenous and Moravian was to be literate—to be Indigenous and Catholic was to be functionally illiterate. Therefore, Inuit began writing diaries while Innu did not.

Until fairly recently, those Innu who did go beyond elementary school were sent far away to St. John's, boys to the notorious Mount Cashel Orphanage and girls to Belvedere Orphanage or later to McAuley Hall. Educated Innu were removed from their communities and were not in a position to influence others to become literate in their own language. Furthermore, while some priests spoke a little Innu-aimun, there was no concerted effort on the part of the Roman Catholic priests to learn Innu-aimun as the Moravians had learned Inuttitut, nor did the Catholic priests have families to help them integrate into the communities as did the Hettasches and other Moravian missionaries. The gap between the Roman Catholic missionaries and their parishioners was considerable.

This situation began to change dramatically by the 1980s. Several decades earlier, during the 1950s, industrial development and government pressure combined to force the Innu into the communities of Davis Inlet and North West River. Over the next thirty years, many Innu spent part of the year in the bush but usually lived in the settlements where the children attended school. Time in the country was a badly needed break from the pressures of a new, unhealthy, and generally unhappy European lifestyle. For the most part, the situation was one the Innu felt helpless to alter. However, in the 1980s, when low-flying jets began invading what remained of their hunting grounds, the Innu rose up and took action.

According to the NATO forces who used the airstrips at Goose Bay, the low-level flights had no adverse impact on the wildlife, but according to Daniel Ashini and many others, the noise of the jet bombers destroyed the peace of mind of the Innu, terrified their children, frightened the animals, and polluted the waterways. Slowly, their anger over this further destruction of their culture built up into rage and in a surprisingly peaceful protest, the Innu invaded the air base, camped on the bombing ranges, went to jail, and solicited the help of sympathetic people from around the world. Ultimately, political activism succeeded in triggering an outpouring of literature in a way that conversion to Christianity had not.

At first, most of the feelings and opinions of the Innu were channeled to the public through journalists like Marie Wadden, whose book *Nitassinan* quoted Innu protestors within the context of her own observations of the situation, but eventually, as the Innu learned how powerful their voices were, they began to write and publish their own material. Leaders like Ben Michel, Bart Jack, and Rose Gregoire, who had translated and published Innu legends when they were in high school, began using the press themselves to further their political and social aims. Newspapers and newsletters began appearing in Innu-aimun as well as English, addressing not just the invading *akenashau*, but directed at their own people, educating them about the protests and the land claims process that had finally begun to elicit serious attention from the various levels of government.

The turning point came with a tragedy in Davis Inlet. In 1992, six Mushuau Innu children died in a house fire while their parents were next door at a drinking party. Both adults were subsequently charged with child abandonment, and when the federal government refused to hold a public inquiry into the circumstances that led to the deaths, the Innu Nation and the Mushuau Innu Band Council went ahead with their own public forum. The resulting report compiled by Camille Fouillard, titled *Gathering Voices: Finding Strength to Help Our Children*, was an accumulation of personal testimony, poetry, photographs, drawings, and statistics, all of it originating with the Innu, and all of it presented in both English and Innu-aimun. The importance of *Gathering Voices* cannot be overestimated. The Innu of Labrador took enormous pride in what was essentially their first book—a book that was planned, written, and published by them in their own language, a book that explained their situation not only to the rest of the world but to one another.

A number of other Innu books, such as *It's Like the Legend: Innu Women's Voices*, edited by Nympha Byrne and Fouillard, and *Beneath the Blanket* by Kistinis (Christine Poker), and many, many Innu stories and articles in newsletters, such as *Innu Teuenikan Tipatshimun* (*Innu Drum News*) and the *Natuashish News*, have appeared since the publication of *Gathering Voices*, usually with the aid of non-Innu editors, but the Innu are now going back and retracing the literary steps they had skipped when they first burst into print. When they were writing from prison cells, political material was the driving force, but diaries and autobiographies are coming to the fore now. George Rich's autobiography, *Struggling with My Soul,* was first published online in 1990. He wrote the book as part of an adult literacy program that he was attending, and is now working on a second book. *Caribou Hunter,* the life of Mathieu Mestokosho as recorded by Serge Bouchard, came out in French in 2004 and in English in 2006, and *I Dreamed the Animals,* the life of Kaniuekutat (John Poker), recorded by Georg Henriksen, was published in 2009. Both the latter are oral works, recorded and edited by European anthropologists.

Of particular interest is the publication of the diaries of Innu elder and activist Tshaukuesh (Dr. Elizabeth Penashue). Up until now, almost the only spontaneously Innu-authored material available from a written rather than an oral tradition has been political essays. When Tshaukuesh began keeping diaries during the low-level flying protests of the 1980s, she spoke almost no English and did not think of the diaries as a potential source of publications. Although there are dates on the entries, there are rarely place names, nor are non-Innu individuals named, as she was generally unable to remember or write names in English. The entries trace her increasing activism, her visits to other countries, court appearances, and other political activities, as well as domestic information such as how to cook a porcupine ("First catch your porcupine . . ."). She records information about life on the land, although not in any systematic way. Often, the entries are simply expressions of her fears and worries related to travelling and appearing in public, and the stress that her actions created within the family. Occasionally, entries take the form of letters to various family members, or lists such as who was in jail at a certain time, or who had lost a family member to suicide. It is often impossible to tell where she is writing from or what the occasions were.

As the mother of nine children and numerous grandchildren and great-grandchildren (51 at last count), Tshaukuesh rarely has the time or the privacy to write. Often her early diary entries were made on planes, and when she was in the country, a recurring theme was "I brought too many grandchildren," meaning she has to look after them and has no time to write. She could frequently be seen in Goose Bay sitting in her husband's truck, writing her diaries while he was in a shop or dealing with issues related to his job.

A typical entry, in this case from November of 1992, reads as follows: "This morning, we took the plane at noon. Now it's twelve-thirty in the morning. I'm still in the plane. I find this very hard and I'm very scared." Further along in the diary, it becomes clear that she was on her way to Brentwood, a treatment centre for alcoholics and addicts, in Windsor, Ontario. The time that Tshaukuesh and her husband spent at Brentwood was enormously important for both of them, but the diary entries from that time are jagged and disjointed. One of her sons comes to visit, but she doesn't say which one—she knew which son it was, so there was no need to record it, but there apparently was a need to write down the enormous relief she felt at the prospect of having someone with her who spoke her language.

Frequently, the diary entries are expressions of faith in God. For example, on October 25, 1992, Tshaukuesh writes: "We're aboard the plane; I'm really scared. I've flown several times now but I can't help being scared in a plane, but I have great confidence in prayer and I have confidence in God. I know he helps me and gives me courage. When I ask God for something, sometimes he grants it to me, he is a person of great tenderness . . . During all the trips I've done by plane, it's always been good weather, there were only a few clouds and there was no wind. That's why I believe God absolutely exists. Whenever I have problems, God takes me in his arms." Often these professions of faith in God are repeated like prayers—useful to the diarist who is praying but of limited relevance to a reader.

The personal diaries of a woman like Tshaukuesh are of enormous interest to anthropologists, political activists, addictions counsellors, her numerous admirers, and other Innu who would like to know more about the spiritual and political journey she has taken. The problem was, though, how to make these diaries accessible and interesting for the general reader. Tshaukuesh received very little formal education, and at the time she began writing the diaries, she had probably never read a book, as there were none available in Innu-aimun except a few religious tracts and prayer books. In her diaries, she made a specific attempt to document her spiritual condition, such as when she decided to go and spend the night in a solitary prayer vigil in the hills; the account begins, "I took my rosary and my rifle." Many of her diary entries include professions of faith. Prayer books were the only models she had to work with. However, if you did not already know Tshaukuesh's story, many of the diary entries would probably be incomprehensible.

When asked if she knew of any other Innu who kept diaries, Tshaukuesh said she did not, but when asked if she knew anyone at all who kept diaries (the Inuit and settlers across the river, for example), she said that *akenashau* kept journals when they came into the bush with her, and specifically recalled a man named Dan Heap, one of the few *akenashau* supporters whose name she had retained. Heap, a former Anglican minister and then the New Democrat Member of Parliament for Spadina, was active in the low-level flying protests.

As time went on and Tshaukuesh became more sophisticated in her activism, and as she began to see her numerous talks and letters published in translation in newsletters and newspapers, the entries in her diaries become more specific, but they are still far from transparent to the general reader. Yet she eventually came to want to share them with others, to see them turned into a real book. Clearly an editor was necessary, but so was a translator, and finding a translator was not an easy task. There are only about 15,000 Innu in the world. Most of them speak Innu-aimun, but of those 15,000, approximately 2,200 live in Labrador and the rest live in Quebec. Under Quebec law, anyone who has a mother tongue other than French or English must attend school in French, so virtually all Innu on the Quebec side of the border speak French as their second language, while in Labrador, Innu are educated in English. Tshaukuesh herself speaks a Quebec dialect of Innu-aimun, because that is where her father came from, but she does not speak any French. This greatly limited the pool of translators available to work on Tshaukuesh's diaries, and in fact it became necessary to have the first seven exercise books translated first into French. Five of these were then translated from French into English.

The problem of translation is not simple. José Mailhot, in her study of the rules governing the use of Innu names, reported that when she inadvertently used taboo names, she only became aware of her errors when she "compared the translations and transcriptions of interviews done by young bilingual Innu . . . The translators refused to let these nicknames appear in their translations. In some cases they substituted the corresponding English name for the nickname; in others they simply omitted the offending passage." Georg Henriksen, in his introduction to *I Dreamed the Animals: Kaniuekutat*, writes that he could find nobody who was able to transcribe the tapes he made of Kaniuekutat in Innu-aimun, although he was eventually able to find someone to translate them into English. This resulted in the autobiography being published only in English, with no Innu-aimun manuscript available for confirmation or eventual publication.

Henriksen's choice of words is interesting; he wrote that he could not find anyone who was able to transcribe the tapes, not that he could not find anybody willing to do the work. Henriksen has since died, so it is not possible to ask for clarification on this point, but it would seem that any literate Innu-aimun speaker would be able to do the work, but perhaps would not be willing to take on a task that was tedious or possibly even taboo. It is interesting to note that the translator Henriksen eventually employed was George Gregoire, Tshaukuesh's brother, who like her speaks a Quebec form of the Sheshatshiu dialect. Although he married into the Mushuau Innu band, he is not one of them. It is probably also significant that he refused to transcribe the tapes into Innu-aimun, but was willing to render them in English. Similarly, Tshaukuesh was not able to find anyone from her own community willing to translate her diaries into English, although several of her own university-educated children were quite capable of doing it.

Innu-aimun has for many years now been used as a political tool by Innu activists and leaders. My husband, John Joy, who as a lawyer did extensive work for the Mushuau Innu band, has speculated that it has been their greatest weapon in their struggle for self-government. "If you have a secret language, why would you let anyone in, especially when most outsiders don't want to be let in? By refusing to cooperate, you are protecting yourself." He noted that Tshaukuesh herself insisted upon using an interpreter long after she was able to address an audience in English, and suggested that by slowing down the process she was able to capture and hold the attention of a predominantly non-Innu audience.

Part of the problem of translation may relate to the sensitive nature of personal material being made public. John eventually became a provincial court judge in Labrador, and he almost always had difficulty finding court interpreters willing to translate personal information that could be the source of embarrassment in a small, closed community. Tshaukuesh's diaries include a lot of material regarding her often-troubled marriage, and possibly this material is considered too personal for public consumption, even though Tshaukuesh herself was willing to have the information made public. It would certainly explain why her children might have been reluctant to take on the task, despite the fact that their parents had both been sober and at peace with one another for many years. Kantuakueshish, Tshaukuesh's husband Francis, was her most ardent supporter and her most willing assistant in all her endeavours, even when he did not entirely agree with her views.

For several years, the diaries languished. A few

of the exercise books were translated into English, some were translated into French and then into English, and others had not been dealt with at all. Fortunately, an interested editor emerged. Dr. Elizabeth Yeoman, a specialist in language teaching and social justice at Memorial University in St. John's, travelled to Labrador to join Tshaukuesh on one of her annual snowshoe treks into the country, and once she was made aware of the diaries, she agreed to work on them. Yeoman speaks several languages, including English and French, and is more familiar with the Innu culture than most people, so while she did not consider herself the ideal editor, she was certainly more capable than anyone else who might have come forward.

Tshaukuesh and Yeoman became immersed in the diaries, using a combination of techniques. The Innu-aimun was laboriously transcribed by a non-Innu typist, and the transcriptions were corrected by Tshaukuesh. Then, because Tshaukuesh did not necessarily write in a standardized dialect, she read the transcription into a recorder, thereby preserving an oral record of the diaries as well as a written one. Yeoman compared the English and French translations and where there appeared to be any discrepancy, she and Tshaukuesh went back to the original transcription in Innu-aimun for clarification. The diary entries themselves were clarified with the addition of material done orally by the two, with Tshaukuesh responding to questions and the editor typing the material into a computer, a form of dictation that Tshaukuesh has used successfully in the past. In a process that Yeoman describes as "rendition" rather than "translation," Tshaukuesh reworked previously untranslated Innu-aimun diaries into her limited English, filling out and explaining what was not clear, Nevertheless, Tshaukuesh herself thought of many of the entries as being discrete stories, and as she revised the works, she fleshed them out so that they could stand alone. She also occasionally wrote what she called "a close"—what Yeoman describes as a "summing up and/or the moral of the story or some kind of comment on the piece." Yeoman posited that perhaps this was because she wrote so many of the entries in a great hurry and in difficult conditions. It was only later that she could reflect on them. For scholarship's sake, these additions were carefully noted so that they could be distinguished from the original diary entries.

The ultimate aim of author and editor was to produce at least two books: one in English, French, and Innu-aimun with photographs, and one more academic book to be determined at a later date. As well, all the material is being preserved in both print form and on tape for future study. It is an enormous and difficult undertaking.

The publication of Tshaukuesh's diaries, which so far have come out in an English-only edition, may be a turning point for Innu literature in Labrador, in part because although such a publication has political and religious content as well as traditional knowledge of the material culture, it is above all a personal exploration of a mature life in transition. The diaries document both spiritual and political awakening, and they provide an account of a woman in a dispossessed matriarchal society finding her courage, her strength, and her voice. Tshaukuesh's diaries are likely to become a courageous model for a new generation of Innu writers, some of whom will use the diary tradition for personal relief and private reflection, but some of whom will probably publish their work also, or use the diary tradition as a basis for an entirely new form of Innu-aimun literature.

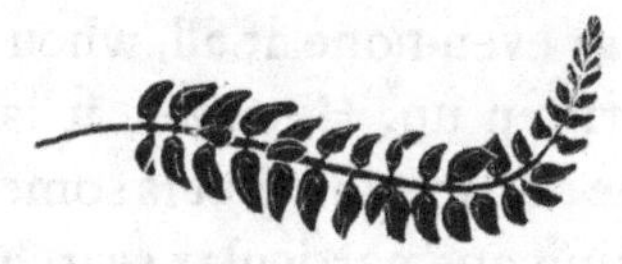

The Mysterious Lambert de Boilieu

2023

Historians, and amateur historians such as myself, often spend many fruitless hours in archives and libraries trying to track down obscure bits of information. These labours often result in only a sentence or two, or even none at all, when the research results are written up. However, it is the journey rather than the destination that is sometimes so satisfying. Tracking one particular search can demonstrate what is involved in uncovering snippets of the past, particularly as it relates to Newfoundland and Labrador history.

Some years ago, when I was doing research on Inuit map making, one source I relied on was a groundbreaking academic monograph by geographers John Spink and D.W. Moodie. The authors suggested that decorated Inuit maps may have served no practical purpose, and that Inuit map makers were unfamiliar with European conventions of map making. Yet when I was able to view one of the maps discussed in the monograph at the American Museum of Natural History, I found that it was drawn on the back of an 1867 U.S. Coastal Survey map and that the "decorations" supplied information omitted in the Survey map. This experience taught me to view original documents whenever possible, rather than transcriptions or reproductions.

The wisdom of getting into an archive and working with original papers and photographs was brought home to me once again when I set out to write about the author Lambert de Boilieu and found myself confronting not one, but two anonymous authors, both of whom appeared to have worked on the same tiny island in Labrador in the same year.

I offer my findings, speculations, and thoughts about these two writers, in part because I think they serve as a warning to readers to be cautious when approaching books written about unfamiliar places such as Labrador. During the coronavirus lockdown of 2020, with all bookstores, libraries, and archives closed, I began rereading books about Labrador that I had read in the past, before I knew very much about the region. I was surprised to discover how differently they read with twelve years of familiarity under my belt. One book in particular not only surprised me, but also puzzled me: Lambert de Boilieu's *Recollections of Labrador Life*, first published in 1861 by Saunders, Otley & Co. in London, and reprinted with editing and notes by Thomas F. Bredin in 1969 for Toronto's Ryerson Press. It was the reprint that sat in one of my bookcases until, in a moment of idle curiosity, I pulled it down and began to reread it.

Recollections of Labrador Life is quite a small book, just 118 pages by de Boilieu and 24 pages of introduction and notes by Bredin, but it is a lively and a charming read, and I was in a mood to be charmed. There were some rather questionable observations in de Boilieu's text that made me wonder if the man was taking the mickey out of his gullible readers, and there were a few short passages that seemed overly familiar considering that it had been at least ten years since I had first read the book, but on the whole I took the work at face value: a memoir by an educated and pious Englishman who had spent some years in the 1850s at Battle Harbour, working for T. and D. Slade of Poole.

The pandemic having brought most businesses and entertainment to a grinding halt, I was given time and space to think about de Boilieu a great deal. The more I thought about the man and his book, the more it puzzled me. Out of curiosity, I had a look in the six volumes of the *Book of Newfoundland*, but found no entry for him. Ditto the *Newfoundland and Labrador Encyclopedia*, the *Dictionary of Newfoundland and Labrador Biography*, O'Flaherty's *The Rock Observed*, and Neary and O'Flaherty's *Part of the Main*. Nor does he show up in W.G. Gosling's *Labrador: Its Discovery, Exploration and Development*. I found him cited in the second edition of the *Dictionary of Newfoundland English* and mentioned in Sean Cadigan's article "Battle Harbour in Transition," but he is merely mentioned and the references are to the 1969 reprint.

In desperation, I turned to the internet, with which I am not particularly familiar, but I thought that anyone who had written such a book would have a footprint of some kind. Again, there was nothing about the man to be found. Google, as is its wont, offered me up several candidates who spelled their last name differently from my target. I located a brief reference to a sixteenth-century French composer named Girard de Beaulieu, erroneously identified as Lambert de Beaulieu, but no Boilieu. I contacted Dr. Graham Skanes, a rare book dealer, who told me that the original publishers, Saunders, Otley & Co., were reputable in their time, but best known for fiction. He also suggested I contact one Lambert Boileau, currently living in Montreal, which I attempted but got no reply.

Nowhere could I find any trace of anyone who might have gone by the name Lambert de Boilieu. He was a ghost, and I began to wonder if his editor, Bredin, had pulled off an elaborate hoax. Bredin, according to the little I found about him, was as his brief biography on the dust-jacket of the Ryerson book asserted, the assistant headmaster of a private school in Winnipeg with two previous books to his credit. He appeared to have no Labrador connection at all, but he did have a Newfoundland connection, in that his daughter had attended Memorial University. I contacted her in New Brunswick, and she was more than willing to answer my questions, but admitted that she had been very young when he published the book. She was so devastated when he died in 1979 that she simply had no idea what happened to his papers. In fact, Kate Bredin was unaware that the book her father had edited was a reprint of an earlier edition; she thought he had found the manuscript in a Manitoba archive.

It was time to go to more experts. Joan Ritcey, former head of the Centre for Newfoundland Studies, said she knew the name but nothing else, and kindly offered to have someone check it out. Staff at the centre came up empty. Dr. Hans Rollmann remembered having read the book, and was able to assure me that there really had been an 1861 edition, and forwarded a digital copy to me which eventually was useful in solving a few minor mysteries. Jacob Bachinger out in Alberta admitted that the book had always perplexed him. "Though it's one of the livelier titles about Labrador," he wrote, "I thought it was riddled with tall tales . . . He's clearly someone to take with a large grain of salt."

Anthony Jenkinson in Sheshatshiu judged that the book "doesn't seem to be egregiously worse than many other accounts from the period," but acknowledged that it has "its fair share of nonsense."

I sat down and read the book for a third time. Dr. Rollmann's digital copy of the original printing allowed me to determine that the footnotes, which contained two egregious errors that could not have originated with someone who had been several years in Labrador, were added by the editor. This third time through, however, at least two of the familiar echoes I had noticed sounded a bit clearer. Bredin, at one point, footnotes a description of an old squaw duck lifted from Cartwright. De Boilieu admits in the text to having read George Cartwright's *Journal of Transactions,* and he uses Cartwright's spelling, such as "gigger" for "jigger," "kyack" for "kayak," and "square phripper" for "squareflipper." With the help of Eva Luther's index to Cartwright's *Journal,* I was able to confirm that de Boilieu lifted whole sections from Cartwright without crediting him.

For example, Cartwright wrote in his Glossary: "Gigger or Jigger. A pair of large hooks fixed back-to-back with some lead run upon the shanks, in the shape of a fish. The Gigger being let down to the bottom, is played by sharp jerks, and such fish as are hooked by it, are enticed by the resemblance of the lead to a real fish." De Boilieu's explanation of a jigger is that "the fishermen use a double hook, cast in a mould, called a 'gigger,' the hooks being fixed back-to-back, with some lead run upon the shanks, in the shape of a fish. The 'gigger,' being let down to the bottom, is played by sharp jerks and many fish are enticed to it by its resemblance to themselves." This unattributed borrowing would have earned any high-school student a rebuke.

I also thought I recognized de Boilieu's anecdote about a drunken magistrate. According to de Boilieu, he was "a retired post-captain in the navy, and the court was held on board a schooner hired for the purpose." I had encountered that drunken magistrate twice before: once on the story boards at the museum in Battle Harbour, which quoted de Boilieu, but again in a slightly different form in Augustus G. Lilly's and Chris Curran's edit of *The Journals of*

George Simms, JP, Vol. II. The original journals were in Lilly's possession, as Simms, who in 1832 was Clerk of the Court of Civil Jurisdiction for the Coast of Labrador and Islands Adjacent, was a relative of Lilly's, and they were not published until 2017, so it was not possible that de Boilieu had read them, although he might have heard about Captain Paterson and simply co-opted the story for his own purposes.

More to the point, de Boilieu claims to have had first-hand experience of this drunken magistrate, but Lilly pointed out that the dates are all wrong, as "there had not been an itinerant court on the Labrador Coast since 1833." Although the de Boilieu description is consistent with Capt. Paterson's court in every detail, Lilly thought that "Unless he was using information provided by someone else, de Boilieu was present in Labrador some thirty years prior to the date of publication of his book."

Emails from other scholars and writers gave me further helpful suggestions. Although the physical description of the island de Boilieu landed at was probably Great Caribou Island (Battle Harbour not really being a harbour, but a tickle between Great Caribou Island and Battle Island), Eva Luther in Fox Harbour focused on de Boilieu's claim that he walked from his unnamed "establishment" to the "esquimaux encampment." He could not have done that from Battle Harbour, but he could have from Cape Charles. However, Lilly pointed out that de Boilieu says "'From the Bay of St. Lewis . . . I took a stroll towards the Esquimaux settlement or encampment...' This suggests he was not starting from Battle Harbour and perhaps says little about where he was based."

Morgen Mills at the Labrador Institute suggested that few researchers use de Boilieu's material, because even the first page smells fishy. De Boilieu claims in the second sentence that he was "not at all particular as to which part of the globe I should visit," which as Morgen writes "is not the way a person winds up in Labrador in 1861 or at any time." She also points out "the tell-tale juxtaposition of precise detail for verisimilitude/illustration [and] the omission of basic detail." De Boilieu gives the day and month but not the year he set sail, and the tonnage of the ship but not its name. Morgen concludes, "I think it's fairly obvious that this is fiction."

Marianne Stopp, the Cultural Resources Advisor for Parks Canada, agrees that "de Boilieu's account is charming, without a doubt, but maddening to use for research because it isn't firmly rooted in place, it's tough to 'follow' him across the landscape, and even the time frame is too uncertain." However, despite her reservations, she grants de Boilieu some credibility because "he seems to have left behind first-hand observations about a time of the year [i.e. the winter] that isn't well-known for southeastern Labrador."

Not all the people I approached had anything to say about de Boilieu. Like some of the other historians I consulted, Sean Cadigan admitted that he didn't remember much about the book. "I looked at it in 1987," he wrote, and "haven't given it a moment's thought since." Gordon Slade, who was for so long on the Board of the Battle Harbour Trust, had heard of de Boilieu but had never read the book.

A few researchers—none of them historians—seem to have accepted de Boilieu at face value. John C. Kennedy cites de Boilieu eleven times in *Encounters: An Anthropological History of Southeastern Labrador*, and quotes him at length with regard to winter houses. He refers to the work as a diary, which it is not; he uses the date of publication, 1861, as the date of de Boilieu's residence in Labrador, though editor Bredin thought it was the 1850s, and it is clear from the text that it was earlier; and he identifies de Boilieu as "having managed the firm of T. and D. Slade at Battle Harbour" although even Bredin does not definitively identify the place or the company he worked for. Laura Kelvin, in her 2011 MA thesis, *The Inuit-Métis of Sandwich Bay: Oral Histories and Archaeology*, refers to de Boilieu as "a superintendent hired by an English firm to manage their Labrador business in the Bay of St. Lewis," which may or may not be close to the truth, but is based solely on Bredin's suggestion.

Folklorist Peter Narváez apparently had no hesitation in using de Boilieu as a source in his work on Newfoundland wakes. He cites him six times in his article "'Tricks and Fun': Subversive Pleasures at Newfoundland Wakes," although he may have misunderstood the location of the wake de Boilieu attended, placing it in Newfoundland rather than

Labrador, and he managed to misspell the author's name "de Boileu." Narváez recognizes that in other cases, someone reporting on Irish-style wakes might be an "unsympathetic sophisticated narrator . . . ridiculing the absurd actions and judgements of inebriates," which reflects de Boilieu's clearly expressed opinion of the Irish, and places him squarely in this role.

Others see de Boilieu as a reliable source of information about Labrador. S. Westfall published a piece in *Natural History* titled "Lambert De Boilieu on the 'Labrador Dog'" in which he uses de Boilieu to trace the development of the breed. When Audrey Hiscock and Linda Braine compiled their *Annotated Bibliography of Newfoundland Materials* for School Libraries for the Department of Education, they recommended *Recollections of Labrador Life* for grades 7 and up. The charm of the writing might make it an appealing book for young readers if it were presented as fiction, but it is described as "Personal experiences in Labrador in the 1850s" giving an "interesting picture of life at that time." Interesting, certainly, but not exactly factual.

Most surprising, perhaps, is Maura Hanrahan, who cited de Boilieu in an article for the *Canadian Journal of Native Studies* in 2000 and again in her report to the Royal Commission on Renewing and Strengthening Our Place in Canada, where she states that "Although there are others, one of the best accounts of early Métis society comes from trader Lambert De Boilieu who spoke of his time in the region as being 'among the Esquimaux' in St. Lewis on the South Coast in the 1860s." Despite what Jenkinson called the book's "fair share of nonsense," Hanrahan apparently is not disturbed by the complete lack of documentation about the man, his tendency to plagiarize, or the scarcity of corroborating detail.

I approached further consideration of *Recollections of Labrador Life* with several hypotheses: de Boilieu was an assumed name; he may have been in Labrador twenty or thirty years earlier than Bredin and others have suggested; and he borrowed stories or created them to make himself seem more adventurous than he was. At the same time, I felt that there were a number of things I could be fairly certain about him. He was English; he was educated; he spent some time in Labrador, most probably on the coast; and he liked to think of himself as a somewhat heroic figure.

The suggestion that de Boilieu was a pseudonym was, at that point, impossible to prove, but it was also impossible to prove that it was not. Gus Lilly tried to track him down through his publisher and managed to find one letter addressed to de Boilieu from Saunders & Otley in the archives at the University of Reading. Dated June 8, 1864 and addressed to "D. Boillieu" from D. Ferguson, it is a reply to a query from de Boilieu regarding royalties. Ferguson explains that the business had "stopped payment" the previous year, and that all their affairs were being settled by the accountants of the firm Coleman, Turquand, Young and Co. of Tokenhouse Yard. There is no place of residence on de Boilieu's letter. Lilly posits that de Boilieu could well have used a pseudonym in dealing with his publisher as well as the public.

The supposition that de Boilieu was in Labrador in the early 1830s, not the 1850s as Bredin suggests, is partly based on Lilly's explanation that there was no itinerant court in Labrador between 1833 and 1861 when the book was published. However, he suggests other evidence for an early 1830s date related to de Boilieu's concern about the lack of a clerical presence in Labrador. De Boilieu claims to have written to the Bishop of Nova Scotia requesting funding to erect a chapel in his community at which he could act as lay reader. Thomas Bredin went to some lengths to try and locate this letter or a copy of a reply to it, with no success whatsoever. He also failed to find such a letter in the Newfoundland archives, though that is possibly because many such documents had been burned in the fires that razed major parts of the city of St. John's.

As Lilly points out, "Newfoundland was part of the Diocese of Nova Scotia until 1839," but came under the control of the Bishop in St. John's after that time. It is highly unlikely that the Bishop of Nova Scotia would have had an interest in funding a church in Labrador in the early 1850s, more than a decade after he had been relieved of responsibility for that district. The Church of England had missions in Labrador at Forteau in 1849, and the first Church of England place of worship was under construction at Battle Harbour in 1850, with Rev. Henry

Disney and Rev. George Hutchinson resident there from 1850 to 1867, suggesting that de Boilieu was not present in those years.

Another clue in favour of the 1830s relates to a visit de Boilieu made to Newfoundland after having his schooner damaged in a gale. When he arrived, he found people were preparing for an election of members for the Legislative Council. As one old skipper told him, "rare fun it will be, for the members are elected by universal suffrage, while scarce a man-jack of the whole electors knows what universal suffrage means." Bredin's endnote says that the 1855 election was to the Assembly, not to the Legislative Council, whose members were appointed, but Gus Lilly notes that there was also a general election in the fall of 1832, when Paterson's court was still working on the Labrador coast. Both the story of the drunken magistrate and the election could have happened at approximately the same time in the 1830s, but not in the 1850s.

I see evidence for my assumption that de Boilieu shaped his adventures—real, borrowed or imagined—to make himself look good, as early in the text as page 1 of *Recollections of Labrador Life*, where he writes that "About 3 A.M. on the 29th of May one of the youngsters of the brig, a few years my junior, happened to slip overboard from the head. Knowing he could not swim, I—who was a good swimmer—did not hesitate, but leapt into the water and after some little difficulty, saved him." I'm not sure I would call jumping off a sailing brig in the ice-infested North Atlantic in late May an act of bravery, but rather an act of foolhardiness. The rest of the book is punctuated with acts of derring-do such as this.

One has to wonder if Bredin, too, suspected that de Boilieu was perhaps gilding the lily in *Recollections*. More to the point, perhaps, Bredin's six-page introduction gives a brief history of the discovery and settlement of Labrador by Europeans, but says nothing whatsoever about de Boilieu or T. and D. Slade of Poole except in his last paragraph, where he says that English firms "like T. and D. Slade of Poole" sent out "superintendents like Lambert de Boilieu to manage their Labrador business, their stores and their hired servants." Bredin is very careful never to say definitively that de Boilieu worked for T. and D. Slade. He claims that 1850 was "the earliest date that de Boilieu could have arrived on the coast," and he did not leave Labrador until 1855 at the earliest, but nowhere does Bredin give his reasons for settling on these dates.

If Bredin suspected some of the information in *Recollections* was less than reliable, he carefully avoids drawing attention to these problems, unlike at least one of the early reviewers of the book. An introduction to three excerpts from the publication appeared in *The Scotsman* in 1862, in which the reviewer describes the work as "a little volume crammed with interesting facts and chronicles which may also be accurate, though they strike those unacquainted with Labrador life as only 'remarkable, if true.'" Some errors, such as de Boilieu's claim that "all the thread used by the Esquimaux in the manufacture of boots, skin dresses, etc., comes from the same source;" i.e. the windpipe of the square flipper seal, or that Inuit clothing lasts from "ten to fifteen years," could be the result of misunderstanding. However, other supposedly direct observations are clearly someone's idea of a joke or tall tale, possibly de Boilieu's or perhaps his informant's.

One example of a tale that is "remarkable, if true," is de Boilieu's observation, on a visit to Sandwich Bay, of a method adopted for bringing wood to the coast from farther up in the hills: "Two flat pieces of board, about six feet long by three inches wide, with a strap in the centre for the feet to go in, are worn by the woodsmen to descend the hill, not the least exertion being used by them. With a heavy load on their backs, I have seen them slide down erect, and at almost railway speed." If some version of skis were really being used in this way, it is another indication that the date of de Boilieu's experiences in Labrador are earlier than the 1850s. The first cambered skis were developed between 1840 and 1850, so de Boilieu is describing skis as they might have been prior to that time. While it is true that technology does take a while to get to Labrador, even today, and these could have been homemade skis, skiing with a turn of wood on your back sounds suicidal at best.

Another example of de Boilieu's questionable veracity is his claim that when a sunbathing seal's breathing hole freezes over, he can still escape the hunter: "He stands as it were on his head, and, using the fore-fins or phrippers as a motive power, whirls himself round at an inconceivable speed. The mouth being open during the rotary motion, acts somehow as an immense auger, and soon penetrates the five or six inches of new formed ice on the surface of the blowing hole."

At least one local historian, Calvin J. Poole writing about Fox Harbour, Labrador, cites de Boilieu and praises his powers of observation and description of the icy seas in the region. In *Recollections*, de Boilieu tells a number of stories intended to show how amiably stupid the Irish were, including an account of a man who attempted to murder his wife by convincing her that near-hanging was an ecstatic experience. De Boileau's Irish were always labelled Paddy and Biddy, but in this one instance he gave them the last name of Glaveen, which is also the name of a cove on the inner side of Fox Harbour. Poole was so taken with this anecdote, which even de Boilieu calls "absurdly improbable," that he plagiarized the plagiarizer.

If de Boilieu was so obviously making up at least some of what he reports in *Recollections*, the obvious question is why some readers, at least initially, accepted what he wrote as fact. Historian Allan Nevins, in the anthology *The Historian as Detective*, has argued that "an artistic lie is sooner swallowed than a clumsy truth." Early reviewers, like that for *The Scotsman*, enjoyed de Boilieu's writing, which *Bell's Life in London* described in 1861 as "a lively, genial style." Some readers, no doubt, accepted what de Boilieu wrote because it confirmed what they already believed; that the average workman is mired in "supreme ignorance;" that the Irish are a "happy, careless race;" that Cartwright was correct when he wrote that the Innu "greedily devour the reeking meal, / And then get drunk, and quarrel, lie and steal." As an academic, Hanrahan is invested in establishing that Inuit settled on the southeastern coast, and since de Boilieu confirms that, she chooses not to notice anything he wrote that might be suspect.

De Boilieu is not alone in his apparent tendency to fake his recollections of time spent in a distant land that is not well known to most readers. Allan Nevins, in "The Case of the Cheating Documents," identifies numerous examples of "fiction dressed...as absolute fact," including Daniel Defoe's *Memoirs of a Cavalier*, Sir John Mandeville's *Travels*, and Parson Weems's *Life of George Washington*. He speculates that people write such documents for money, power, fame, or to create a national mythology, yet apparently de Boilieu got none of these things from *Recollections of Labrador Life*. Nevins goes on to suggest that vanity is often a motive. In reworking an otherwise sparse or boring narrative, "the teller's role becomes a little more witty, heroic, or resourceful." This last suggestion would seem to fit with what de Boilieu tells us of himself. From the first page, when he plunges into the North Atlantic to save a drowning sailor, de Boilieu depicts himself as a cool observer of lesser men, skirting the coast in command of a 40-ton schooner without a casualty, surviving nights in the open, facing down three polar bears in a terrifying stand-off before killing them all at close quarters and coolly walking away, and casually losing an eye to an exploding rifle.

Nevins also asserts that "Sometimes a published book bears frank evidence that the text belongs to two or more very different dates," which is certainly the case for *Recollections*. This, Nevins writes, "is maddening to the historian who never knows whether a statement upon a man or transaction is authentically of the period or embodies later reflection." He goes on to say that "when truth and misstatement are mingled . . . discovery becomes difficult." When fact and fiction are mixed, it is much harder to sieve out the truth from the invention.

If de Boilieu was not in Battle Harbour in the early 1830s, then who was? A manuscript known as the Moss Diary was written at Battle Harbour in 1832, by a man working for the Slades. I was told that the diary itself was too fragile to be handled, but a transcript could be read at The Rooms Provincial Archives in St. John's. After a four-month pandemic closure in 2020, I was able to get an appointment to view it, hoping against hope that the authors of the Moss Diary and *Recollections of Labrador Life* might turn out to be one and the same person. My first surprise was that the archivists were unable to tell me anything at all about the Moss Diary—not who wrote it, nor where it came from, nor even where the transcript was made, nor why it is called the Moss

Diary. However, a cursory review soon revealed that whoever Moss was, he was not the mysterious Lambert de Boilieu.

There are some parallels between the activities of Moss and de Boilieu, such as journeys to nearby settlements and visits from schooner captains and various other travellers. Moss records that on February 18, he "made Thomas Blandford's will," that nine days later "Thomas Blandford departed this life after living on this island as Servant of the Messrs. Slades for 45 years," and that on March 24, he "Sold Thomas Blandford's things by auction." De Boilieu records that he attended the deathbed of "a poor old man whose will I had made the previous year," and then having read the Service for the Burial of the Dead over his remains, "sold his effects by auction, and divided the proceeds as he had desired." Chores such as these might often have fallen to the managers of Slades at Battle Harbour in the course of their service.

Moss makes no reference at any point to matters of religion, he identifies everyone he deals with by name and title if they have one, and his style is completely different from de Boilieu's. Furthermore, there is mention in the entry for February 26 of a Mrs. Moss, and then on September 6, Moss writes that "Mrs. Moss very bad all day, delivered of a little boy a quarter before six in the evening." Although Moss actively supervised work for the Slades, it would appear that he was also a very handy fellow to have around, ready to turn his hand to physical labour also. De Boilieu might have been willing to do some of the chores Moss apparently tackled, but given his social class and education, he is unlikely to have had the skills necessary to carry them out.

It is interesting to note that John C. Kennedy, who did not hesitate to cite de Boilieu as a source of information about Southern Labrador, is initially cautious about using Moss as a source. In his earlier work, *People of the Bays and Headlands,* he cites Moss four times, but introduces his work as "the so-called Moss diary." The "so-called" disappears after that, though from internal evidence it is suggested the author is the husband of Mrs. Moss.

Morgen Mills drew my attention to two diaries known to have been written by William Pearce Moss of Twillingate in the 1850s, and some scholars assume this is the man who wrote the Battle Harbour diary, but William Pearce Moss was only 16 years old in 1854, having been born in 1838. The internet locates dozens of Mosses in Newfoundland, but not one de Boilieu, living or dead, in England or anywhere.

As the pandemic lockdown lengthened, and time slowed, I began to give as much thought to the mysterious Moss as I had to the mysterious de Boilieu, and I was able to obtain a copy of the transcription of the diary from The Rooms for a more leisurely perusal. If Moss wasn't de Boilieu, might there be a hint in the diary as to who was present in the Battle Harbour area at that time and might fit the picture of de Boilieu that I had formed?

Various characters appear in the diary, including a workman J. Pole, a shipwrecked Captain Frederick, and a Mr. Croze, but there are also twelve passing references to the movements and activities of a Mr. Simon. With only three exceptions, the diarist always refers to captains of schooners and such as "Capt." The working men are always referred to by their initials and last name. The title "Mr." is applied to ship owners and merchants, and also to Mr. Simon, who is referred to as "Mr." eleven of the twelve times he appears, suggesting that Simon ranks with the author's social superiors.

Much of the diary records work assigned and completed, fish caught, wood cut, buildings repaired, boats rigged, seals killed, etc. Mr. Simon never seems to do any actual work other than occasional supervision and hunting birds, a chore that de Boilieu particularly enjoyed. On his excursions, Mr. Simon is usually accompanied by one of the captains, and occasionally J. Pole, suggesting that these visits were more for pleasure than for business.

A closer reading of the diary suggests more parallels between the activities of de Boilieu and Mr. Simon than similar accounts of the death of Thomas Blandford or an unnamed "old servant." The elevated social standing Moss suggests for Simon is a good fit for a well-educated remittance man like de Boilieu. Like de Boilieu, Mr. Simon sets a few fox traps, apparently for fun rather than profit. Simon's most frequent "chore" is gunning for ducks and geese, again like de Boilieu. Mr. Simon does a little coasting trade by schooner, as does de Boilieu, and both make social visits to various communities," Mr. Simon to Fox Harbour, Matthew's Cove, and Cape Charles, and de Boilieu to Black Bear Bay, St. Michael's Bay, and Sandwich Bay. All of these communities are to be found in southeastern Labrador and are easily accessible to one another, particularly if you have the use of a schooner, as did both Simon and de Boilieu.

When I suggested these parallels to Gus Lilly, he drew my attention to two appearances of Mr. Simon in the journal of George Simms. Mr. Simon is mentioned in the journal twice: once when he boarded the Labrador Court's schooner *Belinda* and sold marten skins to Simms, an activity with which de Boilieu was very familiar, and again when he gave the court information on American vessels north of Grady Harbour. In other words, Mr. Simon had contact in 1832 with the court of the same drunken magistrate with whom de Boilieu claimed to have had dealings.

The appearance of Mr. Simon in George Simms's *Journals* prompted me to try tracking down further information by searching for Simon rather than Moss. One of the first places I looked was in the indexes for *Them Days* magazine. Two Simons are listed: one an Inuk known as Simon the Fishkiller, and then twelve entries for a Mr. Simon, in three back-to-back issues. Apparently, *Them Days* had published a transcript of the Moss diary under the title "Battle Harbour—1832" that appeared to be more accurate than the one at The Rooms. A note explained that the diary had been submitted by Newton B. Morgan of Kelligrews, who taught in Labrador for eight years between 1938 and 1951.

The discovery of this slightly different version of the diary solved one other small mystery. In his fictional account of Battle Harbour in 1832, *Catucto*, Poole refers to the work as the Moss Diary in his acknowledgements, but in the body of the work he refers to Mr. and Mrs. "Mop," not "Moss." He seems to have got the "Mop" name from the *Them Days* transcript.

Two anomalies still remained. In the Rooms transcript, the diarist writes, "moderate breeze fine weather, Mr. Moss, Capt. Frederick and myself walked down to the Killick stand." In the *Them Days* transcript it is "Mr. Mop, Capt. Frederick & myself." Unless there were two Mr. Mosses or Mr. Mops at Battle Harbour that spring, Moss or Mop could not have been the diarist.

Another anomaly arises from a comparison of the two transcripts. The sole reference to Simon in the transcript at The Rooms which does not refer to him as "Mr." reads, "2 hands gunning (Simon and Pole) brought in 13 birds." By contrast, the *Them Days* transcript reads, ". . . 2 hands gunning. J. Simon & J Pole brought in 13 birds." In the first, Simon seems to be referred to as a "hand," i.e. a workman. In the second, there is a period after "gunning" and the reference to Simon and Pole is not bracketed, possibly separating them from the two gunners. Moreover, the *Them Days* reading gives Simon an initial for his first name.

The problem called for a further appeal to the archivist at The Rooms. A short, explanatory email quickly received a positive response. She had checked the manuscript, judged that it was in good enough shape to be handled cautiously by an experienced researcher, and furthermore she had double-checked the handwriting of the name "Moss." I was correct in thinking that the *Them Days* rendering of "Mop" was a misreading of the somewhat archaic spelling of "Moſs" with what is called a "long s." Obviously, I needed access to the original manuscript.

Armed with the Rooms transcript and the *Them Days* publication, I was finally able to examine the original diary, a small, handstitched exercise book with a charmingly simple drawing of the Slade premises at Battle Harbour on the cover. The handwriting was small but fine enough that a magnifying glass allowed me to get a really good look at the text.

Most disagreements between the transcripts seem to be the result of typographical errors rather than misreadings, and with a few exceptions, the *Them Days* transcript is more accurate than the Rooms version. One of those exceptions is the entry for May 22, which should be as the Rooms transcript renders it, "2 hands gunning (Simon & Pole) brought in 13 birds."

On April 4, The Rooms transcript identifies the two gunners as "M Simon and J. Pole," which *Them Days* renders correctly as "Mr. Simon and J. Pole." However, after a close examination of the handwriting, I understood why The Rooms transcriber made this error. The author of the diary frequently used shortened forms of common words, presumably to save space in the tiny booklet, and one way of doing this was to render Mr. as Mr with a superscript r. Often the r is hardly more than a smudge or a slight stroke of the pen.

Realizing this led me to solve another anomaly: that of the appearance of a second Mr. Moss in the Good Friday entry. "Mr" here has a very firmly drawn r with an upturned tail, a tail such as clearly acts as an "s" elsewhere in the manuscript. So it was not Mr. Moss who accompanied Capt. Frederick and the author down to the killick stand, but Mrs. Moss. This extra excursion with Mrs. Moss gives a little more weight to the notion that Mrs. Moss is the author's wife, and that he is therefore Mr. Moss.

However, all this still left both Mr. Moss and Mr. Simon without first names. The 1832 Slade ledgers for Battle Harbour do not appear to have survived, and there are no clues in the Slade correspondence that I was able to locate for that time. However, there was one more piece of information about the author I was able to glean from the diary: he had a daughter, Sarah Ann. On May 13, 1832, he wrote that he or they "put little Sarah Ann in short clothes for the first time." In Newfoundland and Labrador well into the twentieth century, children were "shortened," or taken out of long clothes and put in dresses or smocks that allowed them to walk, usually at about one or two years of age, although sometimes later depending on how active the child was.

In the Twillingate marriage register, I found an entry for Sarah Ann Moss, who on November 3rd, 1853, married James Roberts, with Robert Moss as one of the witnesses. She would then have been about 23 years old, and the brother born in Battle Harbour on September 6th of the year she was shortened would have been 21. Her parents were listed as John Moss and Elizabeth Pearce Moss. John was born at Blandford, Dorset near Poole, England, moved to Newfoundland when he was seventeen, and had at least one other son, William Pearce Moss, whose diaries for 1854 and 1875-1876 are held in the Special Collections at Memorial University. William Pearce Moss died May 20, 1883 at the age of 44 and his father John Moss died less than three weeks later, on June 5th, age 83 years.

What have I established with the collective research of a dozen Labrador scholars? In a court of law, a civil case requires proof on the balance of probabilities and a criminal case requires proof beyond a reasonable doubt. Given the evidence, I believe that the author of the Moss Diary has been established as John Moss of Twillingate, beyond a reasonable doubt. The fact of de Boilieu's name being a pen name, and the date of de Boilieu's sojourn in Labrador being 1832 rather than the 1850s, I submit, is also beyond a reasonable doubt.

At this point, the identification of Moss's and Simms's Mr. Simon as de Boilieu might or might not have passed the test of balance of probabilities.

I wrote up my findings regarding the identity of the Moss diarist to submit for publication in *Them Days*, and I also sent it to Gus Lilly, who throughout my research on the identity of de Boilieu had been so consistently helpful. I immediately received back an explanation of the "long s" and how to find that symbol on my computer so that I could write it correctly, and almost immediately after, I received the following additional note from Gus Lilly:

> I hadn't noticed before but in the Labrador Court Records transcribed in the *Simms Journal*, p. 226, there appears the case of Robert, David and James Slade *v.* Webber and Whiteway. The case was heard on 13 September 1832 and one John Symon, clerk to the Plaintiffs, gave proof to the Court. I seem to recall that you mentioned a Mr. Simon being mentioned in the Moss Diary, so this must be the same person. Whether he is the Mr. Simon who sold martin skins to Simms at Indian Island Point d'Nore in 1830, p. 9, remains unknown.

Perhaps I'm naïve, but surely only a lawyer could speculate about such a coincidence as a Mr. Simon and a Mr. Symon both having been working for the Slades and appearing at the itinerant Court in 1830 and 1832. In 1830, Mr. Simon sold marten skins to George Simms, who planned to have them made into a muff and tippet for his wife. Mr. Simon's first name and the spelling of his last name were irrelevant to the purchase. However, when in 1832, John Symon gave evidence in a court of law on behalf of his employers, Simms as Clerk of the Court and a magistrate himself would have made it his business to get a first name and to spell the last name correctly.

Having got this far, I sent a summary of my findings to some of the researchers who had helped me, and also sent Gus Lilly's comments about John Symon. Before long I got back a reply from Morgen Mills at the Labrador Institute. Morgen suggested a number of possible candidates named John Symon for the relevant period, but instinct tells me that the first one on her list is the mysterious Lambert de Boilieu:

> John Symon, born about 1802, Middlesex, England (would have been 25 in 1832): according to the 1841 census, he lived at St. Luke, Chelsea, Middlesex with Harriett Symon who was 20 years old (probably his wife whom he would have married well after 1832 given her age): and the census lists his occupation as "Master Mariner."

It is that claim to be a Master Mariner that makes this particular John Symon stand out from the others. De Boilieu wrote, amid a discussion of rendering and shipping of seal oil, the following statement:

> Talking of ships, I may briefly mention . . . that, during my residence in Labrador, I "commanded" a schooner of forty tons; and although a young navigator, I cannot help feeling proud when I remember that for five years I skirted the coast without a casualty.

Clearly de Boilieu took great pleasure in laying claim to being skipper of a seagoing vessel, as did John Symon ten years later. Further research by Morgen Mills turned up other details of Master Mariner John Symon's life, none of them related to Labrador, but none of them inconsistent with an early sojourn in that part of the world.

John Symon, whose name was often spelled Symons or Symonds, was born 19 May, 1802, eventually qualified as a Master Mariner, and in his early thirties married Harriett of the island of St. Helena. They lived at various places in southern England. At age 74 he was retired from the Coast Guard office, and he died sometime between 1881 and 1891, when Harriett was listed as a widow.

I'm not sure it can ever be established with certainty that John Symon of Middlesex was the author of *Recollections of Labrador Life,* but enough of the mystery of that curious book has been uncovered to satisfy at least this puzzled reader.

I wrote at the beginning that there was a lesson to be learned from my experience as a researcher—always try to work with original documents—but there is a second lesson evident here also. Reach out to other interested researchers for help. I found the cooperation and suggestions that came from others invaluable, and I thank them all, particularly Gus Lilly who was so patient with my stumbling efforts at solving one of the many literary mysteries of the history of Newfoundland and Labrador.

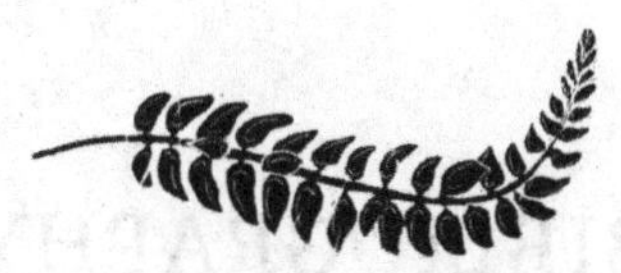

BIBLIOGRAPHY

Labrador, A Reader's Guide draws on Robin McGrath's previously published reviews of the following books.

Anderson, Emma. *The Betrayal of Faith: The Tragic Journey of a Colonial Native Convert.* "A Story That Resonates," *Telegram*, 15 August 2009, F5.

Antane, Nikashant. *Giant's Dream: A Healing Journey Through Nitassinan.* "A Journey Through the Land of Giant," *Telegram*, 21 May 2011, E4.

Bartlett, Bob. *The Last Voyage of the Karluk.* "Spectacular Rescue on CD," *Northeast Avalon Times*, April 2005, 11.

Bartlett, Bob. *The Log of Bob Bartlett.* "Fabulous, Fearful Adventures," *Telegram*, 28 January 2007, B4.

Brice-Bennett, Carol. *Hopedale: Three Ages of a Community in Northern Labrador.* Review in *Newfoundland Quarterly*, Fall 2003, 57-8.

Brown, Dorrie. *Uncommon Clay: The Labradoria Mu-*

ral. "Young Lives Emerge from Moulded Clay," *Telegram*, 27 March 2010, F6.

Bruneau, Stephen. *Icebergs of Newfoundland and Labrador*. "Cool Look at Icebergs." *Northeast Avalon Times*, August 2004, p. 11

Budgell, Anne. *Dear Everybody: A Woman's Journey from Park Avenue to a Labrador Trapline*. "Two Fascinating Profiles and a 'Comic' Tragedy," *Telegram*, 7 December 2013, B23.

Budgell, Leonard. *Arctic Twilight: Leonard Budgell and Canada's Changing North*. "New Books Offer Glimpses of the Past," *Telegram*, 2 January 2010, E4.

Byrne, Nympha, and Camille Fouillard (editors). *It's Like the Legend: Innu Women's Voices*. "It's Like the Legend: Telling It Like It Is," *Portugal Cove-St. Philip's Times*, February 2001, 8.

Chaulk, Aimee (editor). *Snowblind and Seal Finger*, 2nd edition. "Healing Humans and Animals," *Telegram*, 13 June 2015, B7.

Chaulk, Aimee (editor). *Them Days: The Grand River/ Mista-shipu*. "The Tale of a River: Editorial Integrity Unfettered by Nalcor Funding," *Telegram*, 5 October 2013, E4.

Churley, Marilyn. *Shameless: The Fight for Adoption Disclosure and the Search for My Son*. "A Birth Mother's Story," *Telegram*, 9 May 2015, B5.

Coady, Lawrence. *The Lost Canoe: A Labrador Adventure*. "On the Road to Discovery," *Telegram*, 6 July 2008, B4.

Drodge, Eldon. *Jackman: The Courage of Captain William Jackman, One of Newfoundland's Greatest Heroes.* "Writers of Nonfiction Serve Up Excellent Books," *Northeast Avalon Times*, August 2002, 11.

Gimlette, John. *Theatre of Fish: Travels Through Newfoundland and Labrador*. "Author Relies on Stereotypes," *Telegram*, 20 March 2005, B4.

Gregoire, George. *Walk with My Shadow: The Life of an Innu Man*. "Innu Man's Memoir Well Worth Reading," *Telegram*, 23 February 2013, F4.

Grenfell, Wilfred. *Adrift on an Icepan*. "Grenfell's Survival Story Still Fascinating 100 Years Later," *Northeast Avalon Times*, October 2004, 11.

Harper, Kenn. *Thou Shalt Do No Murder*. "In Pursuit of Justice," *Labrador Life* 12.1, Winter 2017-18, 24.

Harper, Kenn. *In Those Days: Collected Writings on Arctic History*. "Two New Titles Well-worth Reading," *Telegram*, 29 March 2014, C16.

Henriksen, Georg and Kaniuekutat. *I Dreamed the Animals: Kaniuekutat: The Life of an Innu Hunter*. Review in *Labrador Life* 10.4, Fall 2009, 28-29.

Hind, Henry Youle. *Explorations in the Interior of the Labrador Peninsula*. "Brothers Explore Labrador," *Telegram*, 16 September 2007, B4.

Hind, William (artist), Gilbert L. Gignac, Mary Jo Hughes, and Andrea Kirkpatrick. *Defiant Beauty: William Hind in the Labrador Peninsula*. "Painter Captured Labrador's Beauty," *Telegram*, 11 November 2007, B4.

Hussey, Greta. *Our Life on Lear's Room Labrador.* "Charming Memoir Recalls Simpler Times," *Telegram*, 13 August 2011, E4.

Igloliorti, Phillip. *I Hope It Don't Rain Tonight.* Review in *Newfoundland and Labrador Studies* 16.2, Fall 2000, 307-309.

Jacobsen, Johan Adrian. *Voyages with the Labrador Eskimos 1880-1881.* "Labrador Innu [sic] Exploited." *Telegram*, 17 May 2014, C1, C5.

Joshua, Titus and Josua Obed. *Memoirs from Northern Labrador.* "Labrador Memoir a Small Treasure Rescued from Oblivion," *Telegram*, 4 October 2014, D7.

Kennedy, John C. *Encounters: An Anthropological History of Southeastern Labrador.* "History Corrected," *Labrador Life* 10.2, Spring 2016, 35-37.

Kurlansky, Mark. *Birdseye: The Adventures of a Curious Man.* "Portraits of Two Interesting Men," *Telegram*, 16 June 2012, F4.

Labrador Institute and Derek Wilton. *The Polar Bear in the Rock: Two Windows on the World.* "Polar Bear Tale Lacks Cultural Context," *Telegram*, 24 April 2010, F6.

Liverman, David. *Killer Snow: Avalanches in Newfoundland and Labrador.* "Winter Warning Worth Heeding," *Telegram*, 20 May 2007, B4.

MacDonald, Martha (editor). *Very Rough Country: Proceedings of the Labrador Explorations Symposium.* "These Boots Were Made for Exploring," *Telegram*, 16 July 2011, E4.

Maggo, Paulus, and Carol Brice-Bennett (editor). *Remembering the Years of My Life: Journeys of a Labrador Inuit Hunter*. Review in *Newfoundland Quarterly*, Fall 2000, 46.

Millman, Lawrence. *Wolverine the Trickster: Labrador Innu Tales*. "Inuit Complexities and Innu Tales," *Telegram*, 19 June 2010, F6.

Moore, Edward Caldwell, and Kirby Walsh (editor). *A Trip to Labrador: Letters and Journals of Edward Caldwell Moore*. "*A Trip to Labrador* a Fascinating Read," *Telegram*, 23 May 2009, F5.

Natcher, David C., Lawrence Felt, and Andrea Procter (editors). *Settlement, Subsistence and Change Among the Labrador Inuit: The Nunatsiavummiut Experience*. "Essays Give Important Information on Life, History of Labrador," *Telegram*, Sept. 7, 2013, E4.

Penny, Josie. *So Few on Earth: A Labrador Metis Woman Remembers*. "A Brave Account, but Phonetics Detract," *Telegram*, 31 December 2010, F4.

Penny, Josie. *On the Goose*. "Second Volume of Memoirs Far Less Compelling than the First," *Telegram*, 19 April 2014, C5.

Rich, George. *Struggling with My Soul*. "Between Two Worlds," *Labrador Life* 11.4, Fall 2017, 38.

Rich, Len. *Bill Bennett: Pioneer Bush Pilot and Outfitter*. "*A Trip to Labrador* a Fascinating Read" (secondary review), *Telegram*, 23 May 2009, F5.

Rivet, France. *In the Footprints of Abraham Ulrikab*.

"Book Adds New Layer to Shameful History," *Telegram*, 27 December 2014, B7.

Rollmann, Hans. *Moravian Beginnings in Labrador: Papers from a Symposium Held in Makkovik and Hopedale.* "Inuit Complexities and Innu Tales," *Telegram*, 19 June 2010, F6.

Sider, Gerald M. *Skin for Skin: Death and Life for Inuit and Innu.* "'A Fresh, Angry Voice' Examines Labrador's Suicide Epidemic," *Telegram*, 12 July 2014.

Smith, Clarissa. *Broken Wings.* "Polar Bear Tale Lacks Cultural Context" (secondary review), *Telegram*, 24 April 2010, F6.

Steele, Gerry. *Bathtubs but No Water: A Tribute to the Mushuau Innu.* "An Intriguing, if Somewhat Slanted, View of the Innu," *Telegram*, 25 February 2012, F4.

Ulrikab, Abraham and Hartmut Lutz. *The Diary of Abraham Ulrikab: Text and Context.* "Diary Recounts Tragedy," *Telegram*, 18 June 2006, B4.

Wadden, Marie. *Where the Pavement Ends: Canada's Aboriginal Recovery Movement and the Urgent Need for Reconciliation.* "On the Road to Discovery," *Telegram*, 6 July 2008, B4.

Zageris, Arnold. *On the Labrador.* "Vivid Photographs Capture the Real Labrador," *Telegram*, 14 June 2014, F8.

*

Labrador, A Reader's Guide also draws on the following previously published articles by Robin McGrath.

"A Boy's Own Labrador." *Labrador Life* 13.3, Summer 2019, 29-33.

"The Diarist Tradition among Labrador Aboriginal People." *Pathways of Creativity in Contemporary Newfoundland and Labrador*, edited by María Jesús Hernáez Lerena, Cambridge Scholars Publishing, 2015, 253-270.

"Identifying the Author of the Moss Diary." *Them Days* 45.4, 2021, 14-16.

"Literary Labrador: From the Sublime to the Ridiculous." *Labrador Life* 14.2, Spring 2020, 32-35.

"Who Was Lambert de Boilieu?" *Them Days* 47.1, 2023, 56-62.

The essay "The Mysterious Lambert de Boilieu" is based on a lecture delivered at the Newfoundland and Labrador Historical Society on 30 March 2023.

NOTES

To assist further reading, the following notes provide additional information on some of the secondary sources referenced in *Labrador, A Reader's Guide*. The notes are ordered by the page number of the original reference.

11-12. Lydia Campbell's "Sketches of Labrador Life" appeared in the *Evening Herald* on 3, 4, 6, 7, 10, 12, 13, 17, 18, 20, and 24 December 1894; and 6 February and 17 May 1895.

32-33. See Stewart Holwell, "Dog Team Mail" (1983), *Them Days*, issue 8.3.

42. See Patrick O'Flaherty, *The Rock Observed: Studies in the Literature of Newfoundland* (1979), page 85.

49. *Kirkus* printed an unsigned review of *The Land God Gave Cain* in November 1958.

61. See Morgen Mills, "Stephen and Florence Tasker and Unromantic Labrador" (2017), *Newfoundland and Labrador Studies*, issue 32.1.

67. Mark Sampson reviewed *The Lava in My Bones* for *Quill and Quire* in December 2012.

70. See William Forbush, *Pomiuk, a Prince of Labrador* (1903).

102. Roberta Buchanan transcribed and annotated Hubbard's diary for publication in *The Woman Who Mapped Labrador: The Life and Expedition Diary of Mina Hubbard* (2005).

115. See James Joyce, *A Portrait of the Artist as a Young Man* (1916).

138. See Ron Rompkey, *Grenfell of Labrador: A Biography* (1991).

168. See *Labrador Diary, 1915-1925: The Gordon Journals* (2003), edited and published by Henry Gordon's spiritual successor in Cartwright, Francis Buckle. The diaries were previously published as *The Labrador Parson* (1972). Buckle also published the diaries of Henry Gordon's wife, Clara, as *Labrador Teacher, 1919-1925: Clara Gordon's journals* (2005).

175. See Margaret Wente, "Oh Danny Boy, Pipe Down" (6 January 2005), *The Globe and Mail*.

177. See Jean Briggs, *Never in Anger: Portrait of an Eskimo Family* (1972).

191-92. These diaries were published in various forms, often as compiled and edited memoirs. Elizabeth Goudie's *Woman of Labrador* (1973) was published by Peter Martin Associates. Lydia Campbell's *Sketches of Labrador Life* (1980), Margaret Baikie's *Labrador Memories: Reflections at Mulligan* (1983), and *The Diary of Thomas L. Blake: 1883-1890* (2000) were all published locally by *Them Days*, and Killick Press released a new edition of *Sketches of Labrador Life* in 2000.

193. See John Murdoch, "Canadian Hunter-Gatherer Adaptive Strategies and Indigenous Language Development" (1985), *International Journal of American Linguistics*, issue 51.4.

210. See John Spink and D.W. Moodie, *Eskimo maps from the Canadian Eastern Arctic* (1972).

212. See Sean Cadigan, "Battle Harbour in Transition" (1990), *Labour/Le Travailleur*, volume 26.

218. See Peter Narváez, "'Tricks and Fun': Subversive Pleasures at Newfoundland Wakes" (1994), *Western Folklore*, issue 53.4.

219. See Maura Hanrahan, "Industrialization and the Politicization of Health in Labrador Métis Society" (2000), *Canadian Journal of Native Studies*, issue 20.2

223. See *The Scotsman*, 20 February 1862.

225. See Calvin J. Poole, *Catucto: Battle Harbour, Labrador, 1832-1833* (1998).

NAMES INDEX

This index lists all people mentioned by name in *Labrador, A Reader's Guide*. Small caps indicate the authors of books that receive dedicated reviews.

PUBLICATIONS INDEX

This index lists all texts and publications referenced in *Labrador, A Reader's Guide*. Small caps indicate books that receive dedicated reviews.

Labrador, A Reader's Guide is Robin McGrath's 25th book. She is the author of seven works of fiction, two volumes of poetry, and three community histories. The following non-fiction titles include Labrador content:

Canadian Inuit Literature:
The Development of a Tradition

All in Together: Rhymes, Songs and Ditties
of Newfoundland and Labrador

The Illustrated Ode to Labrador

Life on the Mista Shipu:
Dispatches from Labrador